For Kieran

And for Bryan,
who explored so many of these trails with us

Contents

Introduction

I magine a place where a river plunges a fifth of the way down a 20-story canyon, where premier trout streams run through picturesque fields and charming woodlands, where bald eagles grace the skies and white-tailed deer graze at twilight, where restored prairies look just as the pioneers saw them, where the Midwest's largest earthen dam holds back a mighty waterway. The place is real: It's called St. Croix County, Wisconsin.

Serving as the main gateway to Wisconsin for Twin Cities residents, St. Croix County is an outdoor recreational mecca. During summers, bicyclists and off-road vehicle enthusiasts ply a number of forested trails while fishermen and canoeists play on waterways and a nationally protected riverway. Come autumn, the roads turn busy with drivers out to enjoy the colorful blaze of autumn leaves. Throughout winter, cross-country skiers, snowshoers and snowmobilists sail across white paths while ice fishing shacks pop up on frozen lakes. And, of course, day and backcountry hikers alike enjoy the county's dozens of miles of trails rambling through verdant scenery.

Geology

Underlying the entire county is 1.1 billion year old bedrock, formed when the North American continent began to split in two. From this rift flowed thousands of feet of lava. In the county, these flows included the area northwest of where the Willow River runs today while the rest of the county mainly contains clastic rock, which is weathered stones that rivers dumped into the rift's depression.

Fast forward a half-billion years. At that time – the Cambrian and Ordovician periods – the county sat in a sea off the edge of North America. Northern Wisconsin was a high coastal area. As rivers carried sediment off these eroding mountains, the sand and silt settled in the sea for more than 100 million years. When sea life grew more complex near the end of that period, their falling shells settled in the sediment, creating the marine limestone underlying much of the county's topsoil. Cliffsides of this rock can be seen today at Willow Falls where the Willow River has cut through it; it can be reached via the **Willow Falls Hill (Gray) Trail** at Willow River State Park.

Two ancient faults during that time offset the rock layers by as much as 400 feet in the county. One fault runs north of Hudson. The other one, known as the Hudson Fault, sits in the state park on the eastern side of Little Falls Lake. You can walk over the latter fault on the **Willow Falls (Blue) Trail**.

Fast forward nearly another half-billion years. About 2.5 million years ago, the Earth entered a series of ice ages. Much of the landscape seen today in St. Croix County exists because of those glaciers. During one of those glacial periods more than 100,000 years ago, an ice sheet engulfed the entire county.

In the last ice age, which ended a mere 8000 years ago, the leading edge of the Superior Lobe of the Laurentide Ice Sheet covered the county's northwestern corner. It formed moraines – ridges of rock and sediment carried by glaciers – and kettle lakes, where melting ice broken from the retreating glacier formed a depression, with the trapped meltwater leaving a waterbody. Moraines are visible on the **Mound (White) Trail** at Willow River State Park and a kettle lake on the **Siem Trail**, located in the Homestead Parklands on Perch Lake.

Most noticeably, the St. Croix River served as a major drainage for meltwater from retreating glaciers with flashfloods scouring out the St. Croix River Valley. The **Hudson Pier**, at Lakefront Park in downtown Hudson, runs to the center of the river valley. During the height of the glacial drainage, the pier would have been a few hundred feet under the river.

Geography

The western third of the county consists mainly of a valley where the St. Croix River runs while the area overlooking it is moderately hilly. The tributaries of the Apple, Willow and Kinnickinnic rivers flow westward there. Collectively known as the St. Croix Valley, this region stretches south into Pierce and north into Polk counties. Willow River State Park near Hudson offers several excellent hikes that are representative of the river valley.

The central third of the county largely is a plain with slightly rolling hills. This region was an outwash plain at the end of a previous ice age. With such little change in elevation, much of it today is prime farmland, but there are a few trails here, most notably the **Kelly Creek Preserve Trail**, which includes a bridge over a stream feeding the Kinnickinnic River.

The eastern third of the county area consists of high-relief hills and valleys that mark the northwestern edges of Wisconsin's western uplands. This hilly terrain is particularly noticeable around Glenwood City, east of Wilson, and north of Spring Valley. A day hike giving a good sense of this landscape is the **Glen Hills East Trail** at Glen Hills County Park.

History

For centuries, Dakota Indians lived in what is now St. Croix County. Shortly before Europeans arrived in the area, the Ojibwe gained control of the area. Trading between the Ojibwe and Frenchmen seeking furs occurred throughout the 1700s, with France claiming the region as part of its empire. The British pushed out the French in 1763, and following the Revolutionary War two decades later, the United States took possession of what is now Wisconsin.

Euro-American settlement of St. Croix County began during the 1830s as homesteaders claimed land. By 1839, steamers began plying the St. Croix River, and a year later the county's first town – Buena Vista – was laid out. Buena Vista changed its named to Hudson 12 years later.

For the next four decades, the St. Croix River served as a major route for ferrying cut pine from northern Wisconsin to sawmills in Hudson and neighboring Stillwater, Minn. Wheat farming dominated the interior. The county's population doubled between 1860 and 1870. New Richmond's **Paperjack Creek and Heritage Center trails** gives a sense of what life was like in the county during that era.

As the 1800s came to a close, the sawmills shut down for the great pineries of the north had been logged off. Railroads crisscrossed the county. Dairying replaced wheat farming; by 1895, the county boasted 14 creameries and seven cheese factories. The **Wildwood Trail** runs on a former rail line past dairy farms that have been in operation since that era.

During the 20th century, roads and motor vehicles gradually surpassed the railroad as the main form of transportation. The new Interstate highway system of the 1950s ran straight through the county, connecting Minneapolis-St. Paul with Madison and Milwaukee to the south. This opened the way for the county's western portion to become bedroom communities for the Twin Cities. In part to ward off potential overdevelopment of the predominantly rural area, the St. Croix National Scenic

Riverway was established in 1968. The **Hudson Pier** takes day hikers into the middle of the riverway's Lake St. Croix to an island.

As the number of family dairy farms declined at the end of the 20th century, the role of commuting – and of tourism – grew in the county. Today, several public areas aimed at preserving natural habitats while offering recreational activities exist throughout the county. Prime examples of this are Willow River State Park, Glen Hills County Park, and a new effort to protect the Kinnickinnic.

Communities

Several small cities dot the county. Most sprung up as agricultural centers, though those closest to the Minnesota border increasingly serve as bedroom communities for the Minneapolis-St. Paul metro area. The county's communities neatly fall into one of three groups based on this transition from farm to bedroom town.

The Great River Road communities sit in the western third of the county, which is rapidly urbanizing. Wis. Hwy. 35, also known as the Great River Road, runs north-south connecting these cities. So also do four major rivers.

The county seat, Hudson, with its neighbor North Hudson, are located where the St. Croix River joins a tributary, the Willow River. Beautiful Willow River State Park sits just east of town; a hike to **Willow Falls** is a must for any visitor to this part of Wisconsin.

North of Hudson is Somerset, which the Apple River flows through on its way to the St. Croix. The city enjoys a colorful history as a rough logging town and bootleg alcohol production center during the Prohibition. One great Somerset hike is the **Parnell Prairie Reserve Trail**.

South of Hudson is River Falls. Partially in neighboring Pierce County, the city is home to the University of Wisconsin-River Falls. Hiking trails abound on the Kinnickinnic River, which flows through town en route to the St. Croix. The most scenic part of the Kinnickinnic is just a mile south of the St. Croix-Pierce county line at **Glen Park.**

The central third of the county is farming country, though the populations of cities along the Interstate 94 and Wis. Hwy. 64 corridors is growing at a faster rate than most other communities in Wisconsin.

The most populous, New Richmond, sits just east of Somerset in the county's north. During 1899, an F5 tornado wiped out the community, killing 117 people. Today, the city is a vibrant town with many great local hiking options.

Much smaller Star Prairie and Deer Park sit to the north and northeast of New Richmond. Roberts is to the south where Wis. Hwy. 65 and I-94 meet. Hammond and then Baldwin, the latter beginning as a railroad town, are east of Roberts on the I-94 corridor. The **Casey Lake Trail** near Baldwin offers an opportunity to see great blue heron near their rookery.

The eastern third of the county is dairy country with cities no larger than a population of 1500, but quality trails can be found there as well. Woodville and Wilson are east of Baldwin off of I-94. Glenwood City is to the north; nearby **Glen Hills County Park** boasts a number of great hikes. The **Wildwood Trail** links Woodville to Spring Valley, home of **Crystal Cave** and the **Eau Galle Recreation Area.**

Attractions

Four major county attractions offer great opportunities for hiking.

The **St. Croix National Scenic Riverway** – whose 252 miles includes the entire length of the county's eastern border – is largely urbanized in this region. A pier and riverwalk in downtown Hudson, however, provide for some fun day walks.

To get back to nature, you'll want to hit any of the three parks centered on reservoirs.

In Hudson, **Willow River State Park** features a 45-foot waterfall that's at the bottom of a 20-story canyon. Upstream, the Willow River is dammed to form Little Falls Lake. A dozen trails can be found in the park. On the county's east side, **Glen Hills County Park** sits southeast of Glenwood City. Several trails ramble around 78-acre Glen Lake, a flowage that keeps Beaver Creek from flooding. To the south near Spring Valley, the **Eau Galle Recreation Area** dams up its namesake river to form Lake George. A number of trails, including an overlook of the dam and reservoir, are located there.

When to Visit

The best months to day hike St. Croix County are May through September. Depending on the year, April and October also can be pleasant.

As with the rest of Wisconsin, summers are humid, especially July and August. Rain can occur during the afternoon even when the morning is sunny, so always check the weather forecast before heading out.

November through March usually is too cold for day hiking. Once snow falls, trails typically are used for cross-country skiing, snowmobiling or snowshoeing. Early spring often means muddy trails thanks to snowmelt and rainfall.

How to Get There

Several major highways offer access to St. Croix County.

From the Minneapolis-St. Paul area, take Interstate 94 east

across the St. Croix River. Visitors from southern Minnesota and Iowa can drive Interstate 35 north to I-94 while those in northern Minnesota can take I-35 or U.S. Hwy. 10 south to I-94. Once in St. Croix County, most of the hiking trails are only a few miles north or south of the freeway. One easy hiking area to reach is **Willow River State Park**, which is just a couple of miles off I-94.

In western Wisconsin take either Wis. Hwy. 35 or U.S. Hwy. 63 to I-94. Hwy. 35 runs through River Falls, past Hudson's downtown pier and riverway, and into Somerset. Hwy. 63 meets I-94 in Baldwin, which boasts the **Casey Lake Wildlife Management Area**.

From eastern Wisconsin and Michigan's Upper Peninsula, head west on Wis. Hwy. 64, Wis. Hwy. 29, or I-94. Hwy. 64 runs through New Richmond and Somerset, passing the latter's **La Grandeur Natural Area**. Hwy. 29 links to I-94 in Eau Claire or can be taken directly to Spring Valley with its **Eau Galle Recreation Area** and **Crystal Cave**. I-94 passes Woodville and offers access to the Glen Hills.

From southern Wisconsin, take I-94 north into the county. The freeway offers access to each St. Croix County community.

Maps

To properly prepare for any hike, you should examine maps before hitting the trail and bring them with you (See the Special Section for more.). No guidebook can reproduce a map as well as the topographical maps or aerial photos that you can find online for free. To that end, a companion website to this book offers printable maps for each listed trail: *https://day hikingtrails.wordpress.com/trail-maps*

Featured Trails

St. Croix County's hiking trails largely can be divided among three geographical areas. The **Great River Road region** is a rapidly urbanizing area paralleling the St. Croix River. It makes up the western third of the county and includes the communities of Hudson, Somerset and River Falls. The **Central region** mainly is farm country, but the cities here – New Richmond, Roberts, Hammond and Baldwin – also are growing at a faster rate than most communities across Wisconsin. The **Eastern region** still is largely untouched by the growth of the Twin Cities and remains primarily farmland and woods.

Great River Road

A mong the most scenic areas of St. Croix County is the Great River Road region. Here the St. Croix River forms the county's eastern boundary with three tributaries – the Apple, the Willow and the Kinnickinnic rivers – flowing to it. The region is so named because Wis. Hwy. 35 – the Great River Road – parallels the St. Croix and connects its three main cities – River Falls, Hudson and Somerset, each of which sport several great trails.

Willow Falls Hill (Gray) Trail
Willow River State Park

A waterfall that many say is among Wisconsin's best awaits day hikers on the Willow Falls Hill (Gray) Trail.

The trail runs about 0.85-miles round trip on Willow Falls State Park's eastern side. Late spring and June mark a great time to hike the trail, as the falls will be in full flow, especially within a day or two of a rainfall.

To reach the trail, take Exit 4 from Interstate 94, heading north on U.S. Hwy. 12 for about 1.6 miles. Follow County Road U for 0.3 miles to County Road A. Drive north, continuing past the main park entrance for about 0.4 miles. Park in the Willow Falls Parking Lot on the road's left/west side. The trailhead leaves from the lot's northwest corner.

For the first 300 feet or so, the trail crosses an open field. Swaths of this region were prairie before settlers arrived, and park officials are allowing this section to return to that natural condition.

In the field, the first trail intersection heads north to an overlook of Willow Falls. Though a scenic view, instead continue straight/west to the falls' base.

The trail enters a wooded area, where it reaches a second intersection, for the Pioneer (Yellow) Trail, which heads to the 100 Campground. Watch the trail markers to make sure you stay on the Willow Falls Hill (Gray) Trail.

Following the intersection, the trail descends a steep hill, taking you into the river valley. Early in the morning and at dusk, you stand a good chance of spotting whitetail deer, eagles, squirrels and chipmunks.

At the hill's bottom, the trail veers north and intersects with the Willow Falls (Blue) Trail. Again, watch for the gray trail markers and head north and then east.

You'll soon hear the roar of the falls and will come alongside the Willow River, as it flows toward the St. Croix River.

In a little more than a hundred feet, the trail arrives at a wooden footbridge that crosses the Willow, and the falls comes into full view.

The Willow River ultimately descends 45 feet over the falls. The main drop is about 15 feet high but more than a hundred feet wide.

A sandstone gorge nestles the falls beneath 200-foot high walls. Geologists estimate the rock at the bottom of the gorge is about 600 million years old and have found trilobite fossils in it.

While the best vistas of the falls and gorge are on the bridge, also cross to its north side, where you can walk down onto the rocks alongside the gorge walls and get a bit closer to the falls. Be careful of slick rocks and small pools that can make the walk slippery and even get your shoes and socks wet.

Willow Falls.

The trail heading north from the bridge is the Burkhardt (Pink) Trail. It heads through a wooded river valley.

After taking in your fill of the falls and gorge, retrace your steps back to the parking lot. Though the trail's short length is seemingly ideal for young children, a steep hill to climb back up after the excitement of seeing the falls will be anticlimactic, so before taking this route, make sure kids are physically fit or that you're willing to carry them. A bench along the way does allow for a convenient rest break.

Knapweed (Orange) Trail
Willow River State Park

Say "Wisconsin" and one usually doesn't think "prairie." But much of the southern portion of the state actually is part of the Great Plains, as are segments of three counties along the

Minnesota border. Most of it the state's grasslands were quickly plowed under and converted to agriculture when pioneers arrived, however.

At Willow River State Park, day hikers can head alongside a project aimed at restoring that missing prairie. The Knapweed Trail, also known as the Orange Trail because of its color on park maps, runs for 0.9 miles one way.

To reach the trail, take Exit 4 from Interstate 94, heading north on U.S. Hwy. 12 for about 1.6 miles. Follow County Road U for 0.3 miles to County Road A.; go right/northeast at this junction. The park entrance road is another two miles on the left/west. Follow the park road to the nature center parking lot. It's about a half-hour drive from downtown St. Paul, Minn.

After entering the park, take the entry road past the park office and the roads to 100 Campground and 200 Campground, and one to the service building. At the Group Camp, turn left/south into the asphalt parking lot; if full, there is a gravel overflow lot on the road's north side.

The trailhead is immediately to the east of the parking lot road. A set of three trails are on the road's south side; take the center one.

The trail heads through about 200 feet of woodland. In another 200 feet or so, you'll reach a T-intersection. Turn left/east.

From there, the trail skirts an old field being restored as prairie. Once returned to grassland, a variety of plants native to Wisconsin will dominate, including big and little bluestem, Canada wild rye, Indian grass, junegrass, needlegrass, northern prairie dropseed, sideoats, switchgrass, and woolgrass. You'll also be able to see a number of forbs, or flowering plants that aren't grasses.

Among the plants you may notice – especially in late June to

Knapweed (Orange) Trail

early July when it blossoms - is the purple knapweed, the trail's namesake. Unfortunately, knapweed is an invasive species that actually threatens the prairie and other ecosystems.

Native to Eastern European, knapweed probably came to North America in the 1800s via alfalfa shipments. In 1980, it was found in a mere 26 Pacific Northwest counties – but just 20 years later it was in 45 states, including Wisconsin.

Knapweed likes dry land, such as prairies, and usually takes roots in disturbed areas like former farm fields. Its roots exude chemicals that prevent other plants from growing.

After a little more than a third of a mile walking alongside the prairie restoration area, the trail veers north back through woodlands between a service building and the park headquarters. If hiking near sunset, listen for great horned owls calling in the pine trees.

In a little more than a quarter mile, the trail crosses the park entry road, so watch for traffic. Then, about a fifth of a mile later, you'll reach the trail's end at the Pioneer (Yellow) Trail junction. The 100 Campground is to your right/east.

You have two options here: Go back the way you came or make a loop of it by taking the Pioneer Trail left/west. The Pioneer Trail is the shorter way to go by about a third of a mile; it heads through woodland, edges the north and west sides of 200 Campground, and then comes to the gravel parking lot immediately north of the lot where your vehicle is parked.

If treating the Knapweed as an out-and-back trail, the hike runs 1.8-miles round trip. The Knapweed-Pioneer loop is about 1.5 miles.

Hidden Ponds (Black) Nature Trail
Willow River State Park

Families can enjoy a fun day of discovering nature with a hike on the Hidden Ponds (Black) Nature Trail at Willow River State Park.

The half-mile interpretive loop is paved, level and out of the

Hidden Ponds (Black) Nature Trail

wind, ideal for young children. Also known as the Black Trail (because of its color on park maps), the walking path is right next to the park's nature center and a short stroll to the park's swimming beach.

To reach the trail, take Exit 4 from Interstate 94, heading north on U.S. Hwy. 12 for about 1.6 miles. Follow County Road U for 0.3 miles to County Road A; go right/northeast at this junction. The park entrance road is another two miles on the left/west. Follow the park road to the nature center parking lot.

The trailhead is next to the nature center at the parking lot's southeast corner. A small stem takes you to the main loop.

Be sure to pick up a guide at the trailhead. Numbered posts run all along the trail and make great opportunities to teach children to learn about the oak forest and wetlands they're passing through.

If quiet, you'll probably run spot white-tail deer along the trail, especially at dusk. Songbirds also are plentiful. In mid-September, blackberries can be found trailside.

After completing the loop, stop in the nature center. Various displays and exhibits focus on west-central Wisconsin's natural and cultural history. A wildflower garden just outside the building offers 20 common species – such as black-eyed Susan, blazing star, and New England aster – and some of them almost always in bloom from spring through autumn.

If heading to the park during summer, check online to see what programs are planned at the nature center. The center is open year around. Also, be forewarned: the nature center has a gift shop.

After the nature center, make a full day of it with a walk over to the Little Falls Lake swimming beach, just a few dozen feet northeast of the parking lot. Be sure to pack bathing suits, towels, and sand toys.

Note: Leashed pets are not allowed on the Hidden Ponds Nature Trail, though they may be taken on other park trails.

Trout Brook (Purple) Trail
Willow River State Park

Day hikers can amble alongside a popular trout stream on the Trout Brook (Purple) Trail at Willow River State Park.

A stem and three stacked loops, the trail offers a several hiking options to meet a variety of fitness levels. The majority of the trail is flat and well-maintained.

To reach the trailhead, from Interstate 94 take Exit 4 and head north on U.S. Hwy. 12 for about 1.6 miles. When Hwy. 12 turns east, continue straight on County Road U for about 0.3 miles to County Road A, where you'll drive for another 1.5 miles. Turn left/west into Willow River's main entrance and follow the park road to a set of three parking lots at its terminus.

The trail can be accessed from the west side of the southern and middle parking lots. Look for the purple trail blaze – the trail starts at the western terminus of the Little Falls (Green) Trail – and crosses the entry road. The wide trail enters a woods of mixed northern hardwoods and roughly parallels the Willow River.

In 0.08 miles, the path junctions with the Oak Ridge (Brown) Trail. Continue straight, passing a small wetlands on its south side.

Once you hear the rush of the river over rapids, the path is coming up on a footbridge that marks the southern end of the Nelson Farm (Silver) Trail, which heads north. The footbridge is at 0.62 miles from the trailhead. Additional rapids are west of the bridge. Keep an eye out for snapping turtles along the way.

The Trout Brook (Purple) Trail marks an excellent route for watching birds of all varieties. More than 90 unique species ranging from songbirds to water fowl and even a few raptors have been spotted on the trail. Great blue heron and ducks are common.

Don't be surprised if you also see white-trailed deer along the way. They like the cover and feeding grounds offered by the oak forest to the trail's south and east.

At 0.72 miles from the trailhead, you'll reach the middle of three stacked loops. They are named here the Western, Middle and Eastern loops based on their compass direction.

Western Loop

From the stem trail, go right/west to the part of the path that accesses both the Western and the Middle loops. In 0.08 miles, the trail junctions with the Western Loop, which heads back to a section of the Willow River known as The Race. At one time, this section of the Willow was a premier trout fishing stream.

Today, brown trout, smallmouth bass and bluegill dominate the Willow. Though like so many other rivers long past its peak trout days, you still can spy a fly fisher out on the banks.

The "three sides" of the western loop run 0.47 miles. They junction on the western side of the middle loop; take the middle loop left/north for 0.17 miles to reach the stem trail and return to the lot.

Middle Loop

To do the Middle Loop, from the stem trail simply avoid turning on any of the junctions and stay on the walking path. This route runs 0.84 miles before returning to the stem trail.

Eastern Loop

Going left/east from the stem trail onto the Middle Loop provides access to the Eastern Loop.

In 0.1 miles from the stem trail, the path reaches the jun-

Trout Brook (Purple) Trail

ction with the Eastern Loop; head left/east onto it. The amoeba-shaped loops runs 0.75 miles and briefly touches the western side of the aforementioned wetlands.

When the trail junctions again with the Middle Loop, go right/north onto it. In 0.27 miles, you'll reach the stem trail.

Of course, depending on your energy levels, the loops can be combined in a variety of ways to lengthen the walk. Or the loops can be skipped altogether; arguably, the prettiest part of the walk is the stem trail, which if done on its own runs 1.44-miles round trip.

Nelson Farm (Silver) Trail
Willow River State Park

A new trail in Willow River State Park recently opened a large swatch of previously inaccessible green space to the public.

The Nelson Farm (Silver) Trail, unveiled in summer 2012, runs 5.7-miles one way. It nicely links the park's developed southwest side to its northeast corner, where a popular trail heads to Willow Falls, the park's centerpiece.

Given the length and access points, day hiking Nelson Farm (Silver) Trail is best broken into three segments.

Trailheads for the three segments described below all are located along 115th Avenue, aka River Road. To reach them, take Exit 4 on Interstate 94, and head north on U.S. Hwy. 12 for about 1.6 miles. Go County Road U for about 0.3 miles to County Road A, where you'll continue past the park's main entrance. After passing through the tiny village of Burkhardt, turn left/northwest onto County Road I then left/west onto 115th Avenue/River Road.

West Segment

The trail's western segment leads to a bridge overlooking the Willow River.

Reach the trailhead from 115th Avenue/River Road by turning left/south onto Nelson Farm Road. In about a half-mile is the Nelson Farm Parking Lot on the right/west side. The trail leaves from the lot's southeast corner; go right/southwest onto it for a 3.6-miles round trip.

The wide jeep trail curves up a knoll into a woods. Little more than a third of a way to the turnaround point, the trail crosses an open field with a steep hill.

The last third of the hike to the destination heads again through a woods as approaching the river.

In just under two miles from the parking lot, the trail ends at a bridge that crosses the Willow River, offering scenic views. On the bridge's south side is the Trout Brook (Purple) Trail.

Nelson Farm (Silver) Trail

Center Segment

The central portion of the trail leads to a scenic overview of Little Falls Lake.

Reach the trailhead by parking in Nelson Farm Parking Lot, as with the West Segment, except go left/northeast on the trail. The segment runs about 3.6-miles round trip.

Upon leaving the parking lot, the trail briefly passes through open prairie, but most of the route is lined with mixed hardwoods.

About half-way to turnaround point, after climbing a steep hill, the trail reaches a scenic overlook of Little Falls Lake. Formed by backing up the Willow River at Little Falls Dam, the lake covers 140 acres and reaches a maximum depth of 18 feet. Largemouth bass is abundant in the lake, but northern pike, panfish and smallmouth bass also thrive there.

From the overlook, the trail makes a steep descent. The next trail intersection is a stem leading to River Road Hunter's parking lot; turn around at the intersection and retrace your steps back to the Nelson Farm lot.

East Segment

Impressive Willow Falls awaits day hikers on the trail's eastern section.

To reach the trailhead, take 115th Avenue/River Road to the River Road Hunter's parking lot. The 4.2-miles round trip trail leaves from the lot's south side, heading into the woods.

This is the stem leading to the main trail, which is reached at the first intersection. From there, go left/south.

Initially, the trail is a steep hill. The good news is the entire trail is forested, providing much appreciated shade on sunny days. The trail heads to the Willow River's north shore, upstream from Little Falls Lake.

Next the path intersects and ends at the Burkhardt (Pink) Trail. Walk a few hundred feet south and down a stairs on the Burkhardt, though, and at the footbridge you'll come to Willow Falls, a set of cascades that drops 45 feet with gorge walls rising 200 feet above the water.

The route on the south side of the bridge is the Willows Falls Hill (Gray) Trail.

Parnell Prairie Reserve loops

Hikers at the Parnell Prairie Preserve west of Somerset can see an ecosystem in the making as a long-abandoned dump is reclaimed. In fact, you might consider repeated trips here during the years ahead to watch the prairie spring alive.

The preserve is fairly new, opening in 2010 as a park jointly operated by the Township and Village of Somerset. In all, you'll walk less than a half-mile on its trails, though there are some side loops that allow you to add a few extra steps if you're up to it.

As you're walking across an open meadow, there's little sun cover; because of this, morning and early evening are best for hiking. Regardless the time of day, though, you'll definitely want to bring a hat. The preserve is open 5 a.m.-10 p.m. daily.

To reach the prairie, from Somerset head west/south on Wis. Hwy. 64. At the village's edge, turn left/west onto 180th Avenue. In about 2.5 miles at 38th Street, 180th Avenue goes right/north. At the tee intersection, go right/east onto 44th Street, which curves and becomes 45th Street.

As the road straightens, turn right into the parking lot.

None of the trails are named and are mainly loops sharing common segments. You'll find getting lost difficult, though; the preserve is an open area and largely bordered by trees.

The trailhead of this recommended hike is at the northeast corner of the parking lot and goes straight east into the prairie. Mowed trails cross rolling terrain.

For 21 years – from 1967-88 – this site served as the Somerset "town dump." The area previously had been farmed by Albert "Alley" Parnell, whose forefathers were among this region's original pioneer families. After the dump closed, officials covered the 5.5-acre refuse site with two feet of fine-grained soils and then six inches of topsoil. The land sat vacant for several years, then in 2010, the U.S. Fish and Wildlife Service began restoring the prairie.

In about 250 feet, the trail comes to a junction. Go left/northeast with the trail curving to the preserve's north side. As walking, you may notice the dirt beneath the grass is particularly poor for Wisconsin. This medium textured and moderately coarse soil is typical of outwash plains created as the glaciers retreated from this area some 10,000 years ago.

After about 200 feet, you'll come to another junction. This time, go right/southeast for 150 feet. The soil and flat terrain make good growing conditions for cool season prairie grasses. The current restoration plan calls for making the entire area look like some of the small prairie remnants along the railroad tracks bordering the preserve's south side.

At the next junction, go right/south. This takes you to roughly the center of the preserve. After 100 feet, the trail swerves northeast.

The area specifically is a dry mesic prairie, in which tall species such as big bluestem and Indian grass typically dominate. Herbs also are commonplace. Such prairies used to run all through southern Wisconsin, but most were plowed under decades ago for farmland. Less than 1 percent of the state's dry mesic prairies remain.

In 400 more feet, you'll arrive at another junction. You're now at the preserve's eastern edge. Turn right/southwest to begin the loop back home.

Though the restoration has only begun, you'll probably spot some of the animals that typically live in a dry mesic area. Butterflies are abundant in summertime. Among the many birds are barn owls, bobolinks, dickcissel, Eastern and Western meadowlarks, grasshopper sparrow, greater prairie-chicken, Henslow's sparrow, and the upland sandpiper. Common mammals include Franklin's ground squirrel, prairie vole, and the white-tailed jackrabbit.

For the next 750 feet or so, the trail meanders but roughly parallels the preserve's eastern and southern woodline of pines. At the junction, go left/west (i.e. straight). The trail curves toward the woodline; if a sunny day, you're likely to get some good cover here, and your location gives you a good, broad view of the sweeping meadow.

When the restoration is completed, the prairie likely will appear just as it did in the mid-1800s to Parnell's ancestors and other pioneers of this area. Indeed, a government survey report from August 1847 reports that the area's southern edge was void of trees and had second-rate soil.

After another 300 feet, the trail curves north. It's another 150 feet or so to the parking lot.

Kelly Creek Preserve Trail
Kelly Creek Preserve

Day hikers can enjoy a walk through a meadow to a pictur-esque spring-fed creek northeast of River Falls.

The 0.3-miles round trip Kelly Creek Preserve Trail runs through property owned by the Kinnickinnic River Land Trust. The 70-acre preserve is open to the public.

To reach the preserve, from River Falls, take Wis. Hwy. 65 north (alternately, from Interstate 94, at Exit 10 take Hwy. 65 south). Turn east onto County Road J. Drive about 1.5 miles and turn right/south onto a gravel road. In a little less than a third of a mile, a parking lot is on the road's tight/west side.

The trail leaves from the lot's west side and heads north through a meadow. Thanks to the prairie flowers and pre-served creek, a number of interesting butterflies and water striders call the preserve home. Among the former are the Eastern Giant Swallowtail, the Eastern Tailed-Blue, the Eastern Tiger Swallowtail, the Peck's Skipper, and the Silver-spotted Skipper; among the former are the Twelve-spotted Skimmer and the Widow Skimmer.

Next the trail curves west and finally turns south as entering a small wooded area that surrounds Kelly Creek. Here the

Kelly Creek Preserve Trail

small creek rises from springs under a limestone outcropping and flows northwest to the nearby Kinnickinnic River, a major tributary of the St. Croix River.

Though diminutive in size, Kelly Creek pours thousands of gallons of cold water per day into the Kinnickinnic, helping ensure the river remains a top-notch trout stream. Indeed, the Kinnickinnic averages 8000 brown and brook trout per mile.

The land trust purchased the area in 1998, restoring the surrounding fields to a native prairie and oak savanna. Besides offering recreational opportunities, the preserve is a mini-laboratory. The nearby University of Wisconsin-River Falls monitors the creek and prairie habitat to help determine the best land management practices for the Kinnickinnic Watershed, which faces pressures from creeping suburban sprawl, population growth, and climate change.

If you have some extra energy upon reaching the creek, it can be crossed. A trail runs along the stream's south side as well as to the far woodline.

Other Great River Road Trails

Hudson

• **Beach Trail** – The 0.4-mile round trip rustic trail at Homestead Parklands on Perch Lake heads around the northeast side of the lake to the swimming beach. From the park entry road, take the left/west to a parking lot; the trail begins north of the lot.

• **Big Bluestem and Little Bluestem trails** – The two trails combine for 0.55-miles through a prairie at the Homestead Parklands on Perch Lake. Park in the fourth lot on the park entry road.

• **Hudson Pier** – At Lakefront Park in downtown Hudson, day hikers can walk a breakwater to an island with a beach in Lake St. Croix. The trip runs about a mile round trip if you can get close parking, which is available along First Street.

• **Oak Savana Trail** – The tiny 0.13-mile trail at Homestead

Parklands on Perch Lake sits next to the playground and is perfect for parents with small children. Use the last lot on the park entry road.

• **Siem Trail** – Located in the Homestead Parklands on Perch Lake, the 1-mile trail starts at a beach and runs along the western side of a kettle – a lake formed several thousand years ago when a retreating glacier left a chunk of ice that depressed the land with the meltwater filling the hole.

• **Ski Club Trail** – The rustic loop runs for about a third of a mile through a small woods at Homestead Parklands on Perch Lake. The trailhead begins at the third lot on the park entry road.

Willow River State Park

• **Burkhardt (Pink) Trail** – A walk alongside a scenic river gorge, a waterfall, and some impressive overlooks await hikers on the Burkhardt Trail. The trail actually is three miles of connecting paths. The trailhead is on the south side of a parking lot off of River Road.

• **Little Falls (Green) Trail** – A pleasant walk alongside a clear blue lake awaits day hikers on the Little Falls Trail. The paved trail skirts the southeastern shore of Little Falls Lake for 0.6 miles one-way (1.2-miles round trip).

• **Mound (White) Trail** – About six miles east of Hudson is an often overlooked section of the state park. The 1.1-mile Mound Trail offers views of the Willow River and a glacial mound (a hill that resisted erosion during the last ice age) on the opposite shore.

• **Oak Ridge (Brown) Trail** – Hikers can learn about geological features created during the last Ice Age on this 1.1-mile trail. It heads from the beach through hardwood forests.

• **Pioneer (Yellow) Trail** – Among the best views of Willow Falls before it drops can be seen from an overlook on the 1.2-mile trail. It also passes the grave sites of the area's first white settlers.

• **Whitetail (Red) Trail** – Expect to spot at least the tracks of whitetail if not the graceful deer itself on this 0.7-mile trail. The path cuts across open fields and along a forest's edge.

• **Willow Falls (Blue) Trail** – An easier but longer trail for reaching the waterfalls than the Willow Falls Hill Trail is this 1-mile route. It follows the Little Falls Lake and Willow River shoreline to the falls but starts from a campground.

River Falls

• **Hoffman Park walking paths** – A number of walking paths crisscross the northern, wooded side of the park. Leave your vehicle at the lot off of Hanson Drive north of East Division Street.

• **Kinnickinnic County Forest trails** – A series of unnamed trails run across 80 acres of pines planted by grade school children during the 1960s. Most of the trails run north-south. The area also is known as the St. Croix County Youth Forest.

• **Whitetail Ridge Trail** – The 4.9-mile singletrack winds through forest. Built for mountain bicycling, the Kinnickinnic Off-Road Cyclists maintains it. Park in the lot off of Whitetail Boulevard, east of Paulson Road.

• For more River Falls area trails also see **Pierce County.**

Somerset

• **La Grandeur Natural Area trail** – This short trail in the La Grandeur Natural Area, located at the village's northeast side, wraps around the water tower and pond to the west. A jeep trail largely skirts the wooded area.

- **St. Croix Prairie Trail** – A 1-mile loop runs through the St. Croix Prairie Waterfowl Production Area east of Somerset. The U.S. Fish and Wildlife Service property is on 95th Street north of 170th Avenue.

Central County

R ising out of the St. Croix River Valley is the largely flat farmland of the county's central area. There are fewer trails here – while pretty countryside, the lack of variety in terrain and the nearness of excellent trails and outdoors rec-reation at Willow River State Park and around Somerset long suppressed interest in marking out walking paths. That's changing, though.

Kinnickinnic Headwaters Trail
Kinnickinnic Headwaters Fish and Wildlife Area and Trumpeter Swan Preserve

Day hikers with a taste for bushwhacking can explore the headwaters of a Class 1 trout stream at the Kinnickinnic Headwaters Fish and Wildlife Area and Trumpeter Swan Preserve.

Located east of Roberts, the two natural areas offer an untamed landscape in a rapidly urbanizing region as the Minneapolis-St. Paul metro area moves eastward. If following old jeep trails (that by midsummer are mostly overgrown), a 1.4-mile round trip walk will take hikers at the FWA through a prairie and along the South Branch of the Kinnickinnic River to the preserve's edge.

To reach the trailhead, from Interstate 94, take Wis. Hwy. 65 north. Turn right/east onto 70th Avenue then go right/south onto 150th Street. A parking lot is on the road's right/west side.

Kinnickinnic Headwaters Trail

The serene fish and wildlife area stretches before the lot. Walk south from the lot's southwest corner to the treeline then head right/west straight along the woodline and through the meadow. The uplands is a restored prairie area, intended to look the way it did before pioneers plowed under the landscape for growing crops.

In about 0.3 miles, the prairie gives way to the banks of the South Branch. To the southwest in the FWA, the branch joins the main Kinnickinnic, which locals have nicknamed the Kinni.

The Kinnickinnic runs 22 miles and is the southernmost tributary to the St. Croix River. Until reaching the city of River Falls to the south, the chilly Kinni is a Class 1 trout stream, known nationally for its brook and brown trout.

Back at the FWA, walk north along the South Branch's wooded shoreline. Groundwater seeps feed the branch and the main river. Songbirds whistling from and woodpeckers tap-tapping on shoreline trees provide for a peaceful setting.

In another 0.3 miles, that sense of being removed from the world of concrete buildings and asphalt parking lots diminishes slightly as the South Branch reaches overhead power lines.

On the branch's northwest side is the 48-acre Trumpeter Swan Preserve that the Kinnickinnic River Land Trust holds an easement on. Consisting of wetlands and planted pine and oak trees, the preserve used to host a trumpeter swan nesting site.

At the power lines, retrace your steps back to the lot.

Paperjack Creek and Heritage Center trails
New Richmond Heritage Center and Paperjack Creek Park

In the city of New Richmond, hikers can combine a walk near a stream with a loop through a historical village and farm that show what life was like in western Wisconsin decades ago.

The New Richmond Heritage Center and Paperjack Creek Trail combine for a roughly mile-long stroll. All of the pathways and trails are well-maintained.

To reach the trailhead, take Wis. Hwy. 65 into New Rich-

Paperjack Creek Trail

mond. Turn east onto Heritage Drive. When the road curves south, turn left/east into the Heritage Center's parking lot.

From the lot, head north to the Heritage Center's historical farm. The barn, granary and Victorian Italianate farmhouse once were the heart of a working farm that since has been paved with streets and become part of the city. Walking past the windmill, though, you'll feel like you've truly stepped back in time.

Due east of the farm, stop at the Pavilion, whose exhibits include pictures of the June 12, 1899, F5 tornado that leveled New Richmond and killed more than 170 people; it's still considered the state's worst tornado. The Pavilion building is modeled after a historic farm machine shed.

From the Pavilion, head south to the Northside House, which was built in 1890 with an addition in 1894. Next to it is a Heritage Church, constructed in 1891.

After the church, walk east then north past the other buildings, which include a 1902 schoolhouse and a general store for countryfolk from 1933. A log barn and a cabin built by immigrants in 1887 round out the heritage center's 12 structures.

Next, head west along the heritage center's north side to behind the farm buildings. Look for a break in the woods where a path descends to a footbridge over Paperjack Creek.

The path enters Paperjack Creek Park, which once was pastureland for the farmstead at the Heritage Center. Today, the park preserves the wetlands surrounding the creek, which was named for a man who lived along its banks and sold rags for a living.

Two trails parallel one another in the park. The first one north of the footbridge is mainly for walking while the other is for bicyclists (though it can be walked as well).

Head right/east onto the footpath. It winds through wetlands and grassy areas and sometimes joins the wider bicycle path. Keep heading east at each intersection.

Eventually the footpath ends altogether. Follow the bicycle path to a section of the park with a playground. At the intersection of East Avenue and Bilmar Street, the trail ends. Retrace your steps back to the farmyard, which you can cut across to the parking lot.

Mary Park Trail

Mary Park, New Richmond

Day hikers can enjoy a walk alongside a placid lake in an urban setting on the Mary Park Trail.

The 0.6-mile round trip trail sits in Mary Park at the southwest end of Mary Park Lake in New Richmond. To reach the trailhead, on Wis. Hwy. 65 in downtown New Richmond turn east onto County Road K/East First Street. Then turn left/north onto North Green Avenue. The road heads into the park.

The trailhead begins at the parking lot's northwest corner.

Mary Lake Park Trail

Paved and wide, the short trail descends alongside the peaceful Willow River, which flows into and then out of Mary Park Lake.

New Richmond owes its motto, "The City Beautiful," to the park. During the 1920s, Stella MacNally donated land to the city for the park, which later garnered sixth place in a More Beautiful America magazine contest.

At sunset, watch for bunny rabbits on the greens. The trail passes two playgrounds, a small beach, and a picnic area. A fun-spirited modern sculpture graces the trail's end.

When the trail reaches the park entry road, turn back and retrace your steps to the parking lot.

Cylon State Wildlife Area Trail
Cylon State Wildlife Area
Day hikers can practice their bushwhacking skills in a major

transition zone between Wisconsin's plant species at the Cylon State Wildlife Area.

The wildlife area offers a rare mix of plants found in both southern and northern Wisconsin. The woods and sedge meadows sit in what biologists call a "tension zone."

To reach the wildlife area, from the village of Deer Park head north on Wis. Hwy. 46. Turn right/east onto County Road H. Between 240th and 250th streets, look for a gravel parking lot on the road's right/south side.

Only primitive trails run through the wildlife area, and there are no clearly marked routes. An old jeep trail does head roughly southwest from the lot's south side through a grasslands, though.

Much of the sedge meadow sits around the North Fork of the Willow River, eight miles of which flow through the wildlife area, and the streams feeding the Willow. Among the dominant plants are broad-leaved white meadowsweet, steeplebush and wire-leaved sedges. Birds often nest in the sedge meadows or near its edges; among those you're likely to spot are the ovenbird, the red-eyed vireo, the broad-winged hawk in the air, and ruffed grouse on the ground.

The jeep trail and the edge of an intermittent stream can be followed about 1100 feet one way to a hardwood forest.

More than half of the wildlife area is hardwoods forest. A variety of oaks can be found there, including bur, Hill's and white, mixed with basswood, and white pine. American elm and red maple dominate the sapling layer. Ironwood is prevalent in the sub-canopy layer with blackberry and hazelnut common shrubs. A variety of ground flora can be spotted here as well, including black snakeroot, enchanter's nightshade, sweet cicely, tick-trefoil, large-flowered trillium, maidenhair fern, wild strawberry, Canada mayflower, and partridge berry.

Cylon State Wildlife Area Trail

The tension zone largely is determined by climate. Temperatures in the wildlife area are just high enough to support the southern plant species but not too hot that the northern species can't prosper.

As with other wildlife areas, there are no facilities. In early summer, the trails become quickly overgrown, so if hiking much past May you will need to don long pants and long-sleeved shirts.

Casey Lake Trail
Casey Lake Wildlife Management Area

Day hikers can sight great blue herons on the Casey Lake Trail north of Baldwin.

The 0.2 miles-round trip trail heads near a rookery for the great blue heron, which is one of Wisconsin's two big birds (the other being the sandhill crane) As the trail is located in a section of the Casey Lake Wildlife Management Area that can be utilized for training bird dogs, it's best hiked April 15-July 31, when the site is closed to such use.

To reach the trail, in Baldwin take U.S. Hwy. 63 north. Turn left/west onto 130th Avenue. Look for a gravel parking lot on the left/south side of the road between 200th and 190th streets.

From the parking lot, take the jeep trail south across a grassy area. It jogs east to a pond that an intermittent stream feeds and runs through. A woodlands surrounds the stream's shoreline.

This habitat is perfect for a great blue heron rookery. The gangly-legged birds are easy to spot – at four feet tall, they often stand motionless in the water waiting to stab at fish and frogs with long, scissors-shaped beaks. They'll also spear snakes, mice and other birds if the opportunity arises.

Seeing a great blue heron fly is an impressive sight. With a 6-foot wingspan, they usually reach speeds of 20+ miles per hour.

If you see dead fish hanging in trees or on the ground, you're probably near a heron nest, as they're messy birds. Look up into the tops of tall trees; their large nests made of sticks often weigh down the branches.

It's best to stay away from a nest, though. Great blue herons have been known to attack intruders by throwing up on them. If that doesn't work, some will resort to puncturing skulls.

If you don't spot a great blue heron, you'll probably see one of many other birds that call the wildlife area home. Among them are blue winged teal, bobolinks, mallards and pheasants.

Two important geographical features make the wildlife area ideal for the great blue heron and these other birds.

First is Casey Lake to the south. With a surface area of 29 acres, the lake can reach a depth of 12 feet. It offers plenty of food to eat and shoreline to nest.

Secondly is the segment of the Western Prairie Habitat Restoration, in which a long-time agricultural field to the trail's east is being converted to native prairie habitat. An expansive effort that includes 15 different locations in St. Croix County and neighboring Polk County, the project aims to restore 20,000 acres to pre-pioneer grasslands, which provide excell-ent nesting sites for bobolinks and pheasants.

Notes: Some maps and documents refer to the state site as the Casey Lake State Wildlife Area. And as with other wild management areas, public facilities are nil.

Other Central County Trails

Baldwin-Hammond
- **Wintergreen Park trails** – Several unnamed walking paths wind through the 32-acre pine and hardwood forest on the town's southwest side. Use the lot in the park's northwest corner off of 60th Avenue west of U.S. Hwy. 63.

New Richmond
- **Doar Park Trail** – About 0.7 miles of trails ramble about the 14.6-acre park, which is being restored to native prairie grasses. The trailhead is on a private road east of 115th Street, just south of Sixth Street West.
- **Doughboy Trail** – The 0.33-mile paved trail runs from the Mill Pond Walk along the Willow River to North Pierce Street south of High Street. Park in the lot west of the New Richmond depot off of High Street.
- **ELC Trail** – The 0.2-mile paved trail links East Sixth Street to Paperjack Elementary School. Park at the northwest end of

the elementary school, off of East 11th Street on weekends or during school vacations.

• **Richmond Way Trail** – The 1.7-mile trail parallels East Richmond Way and briefly West Richmond Way from 140th Street west to County Road A with connector trails. Park along the street.

• **Freedom Park Trail Loop** – Formerly the Hatfield Lake Trail Loop, the 2.4-mile trail circles the park with a long side hugging the shore of Hatfield Lake. Park then pick up the trail at the end of Liberty Drive north of Industrial Boulevard.

• **Hatfield Lake Trail** – The 1-mile trail runs along the south side of Hatfield Lake into Hatfield Park with a spur heading southeast to North Knowles Avenue and Johnson Drive. Parking is in the southeast corner of the Hatfield Park lot.

• **Mill Pond Trail** – The 0.1-mile trail runs across the Willow River dam then partially alongside the small reservoir. Access the trail from West First Street just west of South Knowles Avenue.

• **Monette Park Trail** – A 0.1-mile paved path sits in the neighborhood park and connects to Marshall Road. Park and start the trail at the end of Fifth Street South just west of South Washington Street.

• **Nature Center Trail** – A 0.5-mile trail rambles through woodlands at the 16.5-acre nature along the Willow River. The park is at the corner of Wis. Hwy. 64 and County Road A.

• **North Shore Trail** – The 0.3-mile trail links two ends of North Shore Drive. Use street parking.

• **Rail Bridge Trail** – This 1.7-mile paved trail runs between West Richmond Way and West Sixth Street. Four short connectors link the trail to residential areas and to Wisconsin Indianhead Technical College.

• **Somerset Road Trail** – The paved 0.5-mile trail runs be-

tween Nature Center Park and Victoria Park. The regional hospital is along the trail between the parks.
  • **Willowind Trail** – The paved 0.4-mile trail runs alongside West Eighth Street next to the hospital and then south with spurs. A connector trail links it to Somerset Road Trail.
  • **Woodland Creek Trail** – The 0.5-mile trail heads from County Road A north of Woodland Creek Park to the street Pinewood Trail. The trail is in a residential area.

Roberts
  • **Kinnickinnic River State Fishery Area Trail** – A 0.3-mile round trip path runs to the center of the fishery. On 140th Street, once south of 70th Avenue, take the first gravel road heading west; look for the fishery area sign and turn left/south.
  • **Clapp Waterfowl Production Area** – A 0.36-mile round trip grass path crosses part of the production area to a woodline. A parking lot and the trailhead sit off Kinney Road south of Highlander Trail.

Star Prairie/Deer Park
  • **Prairie Flats North Waterfowl Area** – For a primitive hiking experience, grass paths leave from the parking lot toward and around a pond and the surrounding wetlands. Park in the gravel lot on the north side of County Road H between 90th Street and Thrush Drive.
  • **Stanton County Forest trails** – Trails stacked in two columns run through the 40-acre forest east of South Prairie. Park in the lot off of 185th Street about a mile north of the County Roads H and T intersection.

Eastern County

S t. Croix County's landscape becomes visibly more hilly as leaving the prairie for Wisconsin's driftless area. This geography often led to catastrophic flooding, so during the 20th century dams were constructed with the surrounding region landscaped into public recreation areas. In addition, former railroad tracks recently were converted into a rustic trail.

Glen Hills East Trail
Glen Hills County Park
Tucked within Wisconsin's dairy country is a hilly, wooded region that gives day hikers the chance to get back to nature.

Glen Hills County Park in eastern St. Croix County offers a plethora of trails amid 700 acres of maple and oak hardwoods. The 2-mile round trip Glen Lake East Trail (so christened here for convenience's sake) heads from a vista to a campground.

To reach the park, from U.S. Hwy. 12 in Wilson, take County Road W north. Turn left/north onto Rustic Road 4 then go left/northwest onto Thompson Lane, which dead ends at the parking lot.

The trailhead begins on the lot's southwest corner. Before hitting the trail, though, walk across the grass to the scenic overlook of Glen Lake.

Eight-four-acre Glen Lake is a flowage that controls flooding from Beaver Creek. A dam sits north of the scenic overlook but is nicely shielded by trees. Running 36.4-feet deep, the lake sports largemouth bass, panfish and trout for anglers.

Glen Hills East Trail

The first portion of the trail runs downhill toward the lake. In short order, the trail reaches the lake's shores. It then angles away from the lake and hairpins to the campground's south end.

Along the way, you'll cross three intermittent streams. Keep an eye out for such northern Wisconsin wildlife as white-tailed deer, squirrels, chipmunks and a number of songbirds.

The turnback point is the road Campground Lane. Hikers with a little extra energy, however, can continue the trail by heading down the campground road and picking up a path as it heads along the lake's southeast side.

Glen Hills West Trail
Glen Hills County Park

A pleasant walk through the woods alongside a pretty lake awaits day hikers on the west side of Glen Hills County Park.

To reach the trailhead, from U.S. Hwy. 12 west of Wilson, take Wis. Hwy. 128 north. Turn right/east onto Day Use Road

Glen Hills West Trail

then go right/south onto Picnic Point Lane, which dead ends at a parking lot atop a vista.

The 0.4-mile round trip Glen Lake West Trail begins at the north end of the vista overlooking a swimming beach. Glen Lake is visible from the trail for the first 0.1 miles.

Most of the narrow trail heads through a mixed hardwood forest with a number of red pines. Despite a narrow trunk of only 2-3 feet in diameter, mature red pines soar 80-120 feet high. Often called a Norway pine, they are popular for forest planting because they usually are disease and insect resistant; they're often harvested as pulpwood.

The trail's middle 0.2-miles veers away from the lake. Turn back when the walking path reaches a mowed trail.

Upon returning to the lot, traipse down a small hill to the swimming beach, especially if you have children. Don't forget the sand buckets and shovels!

Wildwood Trail segment

Day hikers can enjoy a rustic walk on a segment of the Wildwood Trail near Woodville.

The seven-mile hiking, biking and snowmobiling trail runs between the communities of Woodville and Spring Valley. Among the most accessible and pleasurable parts of the trail runs 2.3-miles round trip from western Woodville past farm fields.

To reach the trailhead, from downtown Woodville take County Road BB west. Park on the street near the post office then walk along the road about 600 feet west. The trailhead is on County BB's left/south side just past the Solum Drive intersection.

A former railroad right-of-way, St. Paul, Minneapolis and Omaha Railway Company trains used the route until the mid-20th century. In 1970, St. Croix County purchased most of the trail.

The trail segment at Woodville heads into the dairy country for which this part of Wisconsin is so well known. While the path is lined with tall trees and a thick understory, you'll still catch good views of the fields on either side of the trail.

In about 0.1 miles, the trail crosses 250th Street. Shortly after that, a bridge heads over an intermittent stream that flows off the higher elevations to the northwest.

At 0.75 miles into the hike, the trail gradually curves to the east. Where it reaches the middle of that curve and heads directly southeast marks a good spot to turn back. Any farther south brings you close to Interstate 94 and its river of vehicular noise.

Another option for hiking the trail is starting just north of the 250th Avenue and 42nd Street intersection, where there's a gravel parking lot. Going northwest heads past another inter-

Wildwood Trail near Woodville

mittent stream while the southeast route runs through a thick woods.

As a former rail grade, the trail is wide and often open, so be sure to don sunscreen or a brimmed hat. Motorized vehicle traffic – except snowmobiles in winter – are prohibited on the trail.

Eau Galle Dam Trail
Eau Galle Recreation Area

Day hikers can walk across the largest earthen dam in the Midwest on the Eau Galle Dam Trail near Spring Valley.

The 0.8-mile round trip hike sits in the popular Eau Galle Recreation Area, nestled on the borders of St. Croix and Pierce counties. To reach the trailhead, from Spring Valley, head west on Wis. Hwy. 29. In about a mile, turn right/north onto Van

Vista from Eau Galle Dam Trail

Buren Road then right/west onto Eau Galle Dam Road. Next, go right/southwest onto Overlook Road, which curves north; after climbing a hill, turn left into an overlook. Park there.

North of the lot is an overlook where you can take in a view of the 150-acre Eau Galle Reservoir, aka Lake George and on some maps as Spring Valley Lake 64. The view is from the reservoir's south shore northward across the lake's center.

The lake boasts thriving populations of bluegills, crappies, largemouth bass, and sunfish. Anglers often can be spotted on boats and along the shoreline. Recreation here isn't limited to fishing, though. A campground, playgrounds, beaches, and several hiking and equestrian trails also can be found. Many of those amenities are visible from the overlook, which sits at about 160 feet above the lake.

A dirt footpath runs west from the overlook through a wooded area then curves north to another vista of the lake. From there, follow the asphalt road south before curving onto the earthen dam itself.

A rolled-earth and rock-filled dam, the U.S. Army Corps of Engineers' construction holds back the Eau Galle River. The waterway rises out of farm fields just south of Woodville. Fed by a 64-square-mile drainage basin, the river's floods frequently devastated Spring Valley until the dam was built in the mid 1960s. The controlled river eventually makes its way to the Chippewa, which in turn drains into the Mississippi River.

The trail runs the full length of the dam, which is almost 2000 feet. It's fairly wide, but the sides are steep. If heights are a problem for hikers, instead take the footpath to the left/west before crossing the dam; that route heads along the dam's west side to the lake's shoreline.

After crossing the dam, retrace your steps back to the overlook parking lot.

Other Eastern County Trails

Glenwood City
 • **Glen Hills Southwest Trail** – This rustic 1.2-mile round trip route heads through woods, as skirting the Glen Lake's curving, southwest corner at Glen Lake County Park. It runs from the playground on Picnic Point Lane to the campground.

Spring Valley
 • **Northwest Day Use Loop** – The 0.75-mile trail parallels the wooded park road in the Eau Galle Recreational Area. One side runs alongside the scenic Eau Galle River. Park at the lot where Boston Road (east of County Road B) crosses the river.
 • **Overlook Trail** – The 0.76-mile round trip trail heads from an overlook of Lake George (often referred to as the Eau

Galle Reservoir) down to a beach then back up again at the Eau Galle Recreational Area. Park at the overlook off of Eau Galle Dam Road.

• **Pond Trail** – The 0.22-mile loop through a grassy area circles a small L-shaped pond at the Eau Galle Recreational Area. Park at the lot nearest the beach, off of Eau Galle Dam Road.

• **West Ridge Trail/Low Land Trail Loop** – The two paths can be combined into a 1.14-mile lollipop trail that heads from the beach through woodland at the Eau Galle Recreational Area. Park in the lot closest to the beach.

Neighboring Counties

S t. Croix County neighbors several counties that boast great day hikes within a few miles of the border. To the west on the other side of the St. Croix River, is Washington County, Minnesota. Polk County, where Wisconsin's farmland begins to give way to the Northwoods, sits to the north. Heading deeper into central Wisconsin is Dunn County, which is similar in terrain and feel to eastern St. Croix County. To the south is Pierce County, where the St. Croix River ultimately flows into the Mississippi. St. Croix County also shares a tangential boundary with Barron County.

Washington County, Minn.

L ocated along the St. Croix National Scenic Riverway, Minnesota's Washington County offers a number of great day hiking trails. Along the St. Croix River, the county boasts two state parks, including Afton on scenic Lake St. Croix and William O'Brien near Marine on St. Croix. Both parks in-clude river access and trails heading through woodlands and restored prairies. Also on the river or within viewing distance of it are the Carpenter Nature Center (which boasts apple orchards), St. Croix Bluffs Regional Park, and Belwin Conservancy (which cares for a small buffalo herd). In the scenic riverway itself is four-story Fairy Falls and the historic Boom Site with its sandstone formations, both just north of Stillwater.

Kettlekamp Prairie Trail
Belwin Conservancy

An observation tower overlooking a restored prairie awaits day hikers on the Kettlekamp Prairie Trail at the Belwin Conservancy.

Though privately owned, the nature preserve just west of Hudson is open to the public. The Kettlekamp trail runs about 0.75 miles in the conservancy's northwest corner.

To reach the trail, from Interstate 94, head south on Minn. Hwy. 21/Stagecoach Trail (Note that if coming from the east, you'll want to exit onto the wayside and then take a short connector road from its west side to Hwy. 21.). After passing Indian Trail South, turn left/east onto the conservancy's entry

Kettlekamp Prairie Trail

road. At the park's headquarters, go left/north; park where the road ends at the nature center.

The trailhead is at the observation tower near the center's

front. Go right/south onto the trail, which along with red pines rings the Kettlekamp Prairie.

The opening section for the trail descends somewhat but is wide and easily to follow. As it's an open area, you'll definitely need either sunhat or sunscreen.

Kettlekamp is the largest of several open spaces being restored as prairie at Belwin. Well over 150 acres of prairie has been reseeded there.

At around $1000 per acre to replant prairies with a healthy seed mix, Belwin uses a couple of combines to harvest its own land to keep costs down. Seeds come from two major native prairie grasses – Indian grass and big bluestem – as well as a number of flower species can't be obtained that way.

To overcome that problem, Belwin volunteers engage in the ancient practice of seed scavenging – or harvesting the seeds by hand.

During September and October, Belwin hosts a few seed collection events in which Indian grass and big bluestem seeds are picked at the Stagecoach Prairie Natural area. Through the winter, the seeds dry on tarps, then in spring are run through a hammermill so they can be broken into chaff and planted.

As the loop nears its end, you'll have to ascend back toward the tower. Once you've arrived there, take a walk to the tower's top, which offers a great view of the St. Croix River and far Wisconsin shore to the southeast.

North River Trail
Afton State Park

Day hikers can enjoy a pleasant walk alongside the widest section of the St. Croix River on the North River Trail at Minnesota's Afton State Park.

The 2.2-miles round trip also offers the opportunity for a

swim to cool off when the walk is all over.

To reach the park, take Minn. Hwy. 21 about 4.5 miles south of Afton. Turn east into the park at the Minn. Hwy. 20 intersection. Follow the entry road to a set of seven parking lots in front of the visitor center; any one of them will work with a trailhead or a connecting trail on each lot's east side; just always be sure to veer left/north when coming to the first trail junction. If taking the southernmost (first) parking lot along the entry road, you'll add about 0.3 miles one-way to the hike.

The trail gradually veers toward the St. Croix, which at this point on its course is known as Lake St. Croix because of its width. Lake St. Croix stretches south from Stillwater to Prescott, where the river joins the Mississippi.

The river reaches its widest at 1.25 miles just north of the state park. Its deepest point is 78 feet.

Between the parking lot and river, the North River Trail passes picnic areas, a shelter, and telescopes for viewing the scenic Wisconsin side across the sapphire-colored water. The trail goes by the swimming beach about a half-mile to 0.75 miles into the hike.

As the trail stays close to the river below the bluff, trees along the way can be underwater during spring flooding and other high water years.

Once away from the beach, the trail becomes a tranquil, natural path. Your only company likely will be the birds of prey circling for fish and the number of recreational boats enjoying the river.

This section of the river is extremely popular among anglers. More than 60 fish species call Lake St. Croix home; among them are walleye and muskie (Minnesota's and Wisconsin's state fish respectively), northern pike, largemouth and smallmouth bass, bluegill and crappie. White bass is particularly abundant near

Swimming beach on North River Trail

the park.

Some fish size is exceptional. Minnesota's state record cat-fish – coming in at 70 pounds – was caught in Lake St. Croix.

Fishermen also have hauled in lake sturgeon weighing more than 50 pounds. Some channel catfish weigh in excess of 25 pounds.

At 1.1-1.4 miles from the visitor center, the trail veers west away from the river and climbs the hill up the bluff. This marks a good time to turn back. Before returning to your vehicle, stop at the visitor center to learn more about the river and ecosystems at the park.

This also is a bicycle trail, so be aware of the two-wheelers. During spring and early summer, always don repellant for mosquitos, which is Minnesota's unofficial state bird.

Fairy Falls Trail
St. Croix National Scenic Riverway

Day hikers can enjoy a little-known four-story waterfall near Stillwater on the Fairy Falls Trail.

For years, the short quarter-mile round trip was located on private land but is now operated by National Park Service as part of a 55-acre addition to the St. Croix National Scenic Riverway. The Fairy Falls Day Use Area is open 8 a.m.–8 p.m. daily.

To reach the falls, from downtown Stillwater, take Minn. Hwy. 95 north. Turn left/northwest onto Minn. Hwy. 96 then right/north onto County Road 11/Boom Road. The county road separates from Boom Road and goes left/west and becomes Fairy Falls Road North as heading up a hill. Park along the west side of Orwell Avenue, which is directly across from the day use area. The trailhead is a footpath to the right of the yellow directional sign.

The footpath heads through a hardwood forest with a number of birch trees. Be careful of not taking narrow side-paths that meander through the woods away from the falls.

Lip of Fairy Falls

Within about 0.1 miles, the trail reaches the top of the falls, where Silver Creek drops into a deep pool in the gorge below then continues on its way to the St. Croix River. A wooden bridge crosses the creek about a dozen feet from the waterfalls' rim.

The trail can be followed around the gorge's rim, but unless late in fall or early in spring when the foliage is light, the glen isn't visible below. Still, it's a pleasant walk with a few glacial erratics along the way.

You can take a spur trail, tucked against one gorge wall, down to the creek bottom. There are no signs indicating the way to go, but it looks more like a washed out draw than a walking path. Still, it's traversable, though you shouldn't try it during night, when the ground is wet, or with young children. The fall is a long way down.

The bluff sits atop sandstone laid here about 500 million years old during the Cambrian. Floodwaters from melting glaciers swept through the river valley some 8000 years ago at the end of the last ice age, carving out the sandstone, which Silver Creek has further eroded back. Today, the thick beds exposed along the river are known as the "St. Croixian series."

During spring when Silver Creek is higher due to snow melt, those who hike down the bluff's side can feel mist from the falls. There's a shallow cave behind the base of the falls, and if you don't mind getting wet, you can go into it and see the waterfall from the inside.

By early summer, the gorge is thick with greenery. During autumn, look for Jack in the Pulpit; the bright orange berries that lie under the pulpit add another tinge of color to the scene.

During spring and autumn, Silver Creek can be hiked a ways downstream. From the falls, the creek flows about a quarter mile before spilling into the St. Croix.

In days past, the falls flowed heavily through the summer. By the early 1950s, it fell off during late summer, as the lake feeding Silver Creek dried to a wetlands.

The falls and glen – which Native Americans living in the area called Ugua-Wah-to-gi-di-big, or "shadow of the falls" – were popular with local in the 1890s through the early 1900s when hundreds of people would walk there from Stillwater to pick pink crocuses and violets as well as to enjoy picnics. Postcards even were made of the falls.

After the hike, you can add to your day by driving on Hwy. 95 north of County Road 11 to the St. Croix Boom Site Trail, which is a few hundred feet up the highway on the right/east side.

Boom Site Trail

St. Croix National Scenic Riverway

Families can day hike a historical remnant from the St. Croix River's lumber baron days north of Stillwater.

The St. Croix Boom Site Trail runs a mere 0.4 miles round trip but makes for a scenic afternoon diversion. A century-and-a-half-ago ago, the site was a bustling center of activity a where men pulled logs from the St. Croix River and sent them on their way to sawmills.

To reach the trail, from downtown Stillwater drive north on Minn. Hwy. 95. Watch for the signs; after Pawnee Avenue North, there's a turnoff for the Boom Site on the right/east. Park in the looping access road. The trailhead is south of the lot's access road. The Boom Site is merely a 50-foot walk down a staircase to a beach.

Throughout the mid- and late-1800s, lumberjacks downed whole forests across northern Minnesota and Wisconsin, branded each log with the sawmill it was to go to, and floated the timber down the St. Croix River on its way to sawmills.

When the St. Croix Boom Company went bust upstream near Marine on St. Croix, several Stillwater lumber barons bought the business and moved it north of town. The boom company drew the timber from the river then sorted and delivered it to the correct sawmill in Stillwater. All through the 1870s, logs would back up some 15 miles on the river during midsummer as awaiting for the boom company to pull them out.

By the early 20th century, most Northwoods forests were gone, and the boom site ceased operation in 1914. As the economy changed and generations passed, the site was largely forgotten.

The National Park Service discovered it during a 1975 survey while identifying historical sites along the St. Croix.

Today, it's a National Historic Landmark in the St. Croix National Scenic Riverway.

At the bottom of the stairs, hikers can head up and down the pleasant beach below the sandstone bluff. The beach peters out about 600 feet downstream and heads roughly 400 feet upstream to a nice point overlooking a river island.

Riverside Trail
William O'Brien State Park

Day hikers can learn about the power of floods on the St. Croix River via the Riverside Trail at William O'Brien State Park near Marine on St. Croix.

The 1.5-mile trail loops through a floodplain and typically is open during summer and autumn when water levels have gone down. Don't think of this area as a swamp, though – you'll find rest areas (some with benches) about every 900 feet on the trail, as well as interpretive signs.

To reach the trail, from Marine on St. Croix, Minn., take Minn. Hwy. 95 north into the park. Turn right/east onto O'Brien Trail North/County Road 33. The road curves south, dead ending in a parking area alongside Lake Alice. The trail begins at the picnic grounds immediately east of the parking lot.

At the amphitheater, the trail curves east then north again as paralleling a back channel of the St. Croix River. The fresh scent of pine needles upon the trail and the gentle rush of water along the river's rock walls instantly lulls you into a feeling of serenity.

About 0.3 miles from the amphitheater, shortly after passing a stem trail leading to a campground, the back channel joins the main channel. Roughly half of the trail follows the river, mainly through a good mix of hardwoods common to a flood-

Lake Alice on Riverside Trail

plain forest in this region. During autumn, their leaves turn gold, red, orange and brown. Across the water is Wisconsin, and with the two undeveloped shorelines, tranquility reigns.

A little more than halfway through the hike, the trail veers from the river and follows a small stream that flows from the bluffs into the St. Croix. Frogs make their home along the creek in large numbers, and you're likely to hear them through the day.

The trail then curves south and soon crosses O'Brien Trail North. This marks the steepest section of the trail as it rises and drops about 40 feet over a knoll.

Next the trail squeezes between the road and Lake Alice. The lake was named for Alice O'Brien, whose donation of 180 acres in honor of her father, William, launched the park.

Springs at Lake Alice's north end feeds it through the year, assuring the water remains clean and blue all summer. Keep an eye to the sky for eagles and hawks looking for a meal in the lake. Geese and ducks usually can be spotted floating about, so if you have little ones, bring some dried bread they can toss into the water to feed the waterfowl.

The Riverside Trail is wheelchair accessible. It also has restrooms and a swimming area on Lake Alice at trail's end, so be sure to pack your kids' swimming trunks.

Other Washington County Trails

Afton

• **Afton to Lakeland Trail** – The 3.4-mile (one-way) trail connects the communities of Afton and Lakeland. Parking is available near either trailhead, which are on Pike Avenue close to the city hall in Afton and at Crocker Park in Lakeland. The trail parallels County Road 18.

• **Aftonwood Park Walking Path** – A trail runs through the 7.74-acre wooded park, which contains a steep ravine. The park is located between Osgood Avenue and County Road 21.

• **Meadow Ridge Walking Path** – A woodchip path with benches runs through the 10.4-acre Meadow Ridge Park located at the corner of E. Oakgreen Circle and Nybeck Avenue South. Park off of the street.

• **Remus Park Trail** – A gravel trail runs north-south through the 5-acre park, connecting Parsons Court South and Pheasant Court South. Bicycles and horse riding are allowed on the trail.

• **Steamboat Park walking paths** – Undesignated walking paths wind through the 27-acre city park south of the marina and along the St. Croix River. Mature maples, oaks and cottonwoods grow in the park; be aware that parts of it can flood in spring.

Afton State Park

Among the park's best (and named) trails are:

• **Deer Valley Loop** – For a solid workout and great vistas, try this 2.2-mile trail, which heads up and down the bluff overlooking the St. Croix. You'll need to first hike 1.3 miles of connecting trails to reach the trailhead for a 4.8-mile round trip.

• **Prairie Loop** – The 2.1-mile trail circles a blufftop prairie and can be extended by taking loops off the main route. A mile of connecting trails are needed to reach the trailhead for a 4.1-mile round trip.

• **North River Trail** – A tranquil dirt trail runs next to the St. Croix River's widest section. The 2.2-miles round trip also offers the opportunity for a swim to cool off when the walk is all over.

• **South River Trail** – The 3.2-mile round-trip trail rambles alongside the St. Croix River through a woods. It offers great views of the scenic Wisconsin shoreline.

• **Trout Brook Loop** – The trail heads alongside and over Trout Brook, a St. Croix tributary, then behind a small border that borders the stream. Though only 1.5-miles long, you'll need to hike 2.3 miles of connecting trails to its trailhead, resulting in a 6.1-mile round trip.

Belwin Conservancy

Trails in the Bell Oak Savanna and Valley Creek areas, going roughly east to west and then north to south, include:

• **Red Pine Trail** – The 0.12-mile loop through a red pine forest can be picked up at the nature center. Also known as Norway Pine, the majestic and sturdy evergreen that is the trail's namesake is Minnesota's state tree.

• **Tower to Tower Trail** – Starting at the observation tower next to the nature center, the 1.4-miles round trip trail goes through prairie and forest to the Treetop Tower. Its opening section rambles through part of the Kettlekamp Prairie.

- **Bell's Fen Trail** – Heading south from the observation tower, the first segment of this 1.7-mile round trip shares part of the Kettlekamp Prairie Trail. Upon veering south on its own route, it passes a pond and loops through Bell's Fen.
- **Valley Creek Trail** – The 1.2-mile round trip heads south to an overlook of Valley Creek. Take the Red Pine trail south of the nature center to reach the trailhead.
- **White Pine Trail** – A 1.6-mile round trip hike runs through white pines and part of the Postage Stamp Prairie. Spur trails lead to an archeological site and the Treetop Tower. It shares a trailhead with the Valley Creek Trail.
- **Dry Prairie Trail** – A 0.75-mile loop heads through and around Goat Prairie as well as adjoining woodland. A spur trail leads to an observatory at the prairie's north end. Reaching the loop requires taking part of either the Red Pine or the White Pine trails.
- **Bulrush Slough Trail** – Circling around a wetlands, the 0.5-mile trail also crosses the adjoining Deep Pool. The shortest way to reach the trail is a connector trail heading southeast from the conservancy headquarters; connector trails from the Dry Prairie Trail also lead to it.

To view the conservancy's bison:

- **Bison Observation Trail** – A short trail leads along a fence and to a 20-foot high observation platform overlooking a prairie area containing bison at Belwin Conservancy. Parking is available at the trailhead, off of Division Street east of Stagecoach Trail just south of Interstate 94.

Stillwater
- **Brown's Creek Nature Preserve Ski Trail** – The Brown's

Creek Park and Nature Preserve Ski Trail offers among the best day hiking option in the Stillwater area. It gives you a good sense of what a blufftop woodlands area is like. A parking lot is off of County Road 64/McKusick Road North past Maryland Avenue North. The **Browns Creek State Trail**, of which the ski trail is a segment of, also can be picked up on the north side of downtown next to the former depot.

• **Gateway State Trail** – The eastern terminus of the trail begins at Pine Point Regional Park north of Stillwater. A good segment to take is the 4.2 miles from the park to just north of Duluth Junction. Along the way, the trail crosses a creek and boasts two picnic areas. Much of this segment passes farm fields. A fee is charged to enter the park.

Marine on St. Croix

• **Arcola High Bridge Trail** – An undesignated trail in the St. Croix National Scenic Riverway runs 1-mile round trip down a bluff to the a cedar grove and the St. Croix River just below the hundred-year-old railroad bridge. Park in the pullout along Arcola Trail about 3.5 miles east of Minn. Hwy. 95 south of town.

• **Big Marine Park Reserve Trail** – Hikers can enjoy a walk through a woodlands and on a long pier at Big Marine Park Reserve west of town. The unnamed trail in the fairly new Washington County park runs 0.75 miles round-trip.

• **Falls Creek Scientific and Natural Area Trail** – The primitive nature trail runs through several diverse ecosystems atop a St. Croix River Bluff north of town in Chisago County. An access road off of Hwy. 95 directly across from Pilar Road North leads to a parking lot.

• **Jackson Meadows Trails** – Several undesignated stacked loops run through a city-owned woods immediately east of

Jackson Meadow. Pick up the trail at the parking lot on the west side of Jackson Trail near the Sandpiper Lane junction.

• **Old Guslander Trail** – A 0.66-mile trail loops through a city-owned woods adjoining William O'Brien State Park. The trailhead runs north from Old Guslander Trail North just west of the Broadway Street junction west of town; park off the road at the trailhead.

• **Sawmill and Waterfalls Trail** – A 0.25-mile trail heads through the former sight of Minnesota's first commercial saw-mill and past a small waterfall on a creek flowing into the St. Croix River. Park on Judd Street south of Maple Street in town.

• **Square Lake Park beachwalk** – A beach stretches just under 0.25 miles along the eastern shores of a pretty lake at Square Lake Park south of town. Leave your vehicle in the Washington County park's lot just off of County Road 7 south of the County Road 59 junction.

William O'Brien State Park

• **Beaver Lodge Trail** – The 0.7-mile loop encircles a wetlands where beavers have created a small pond; you'll hike 1.7 miles round trip with the connecting trails. Upon reaching the Wedge Hill Savanna Trail, stay on that loop's western side. At the next junction at the bottom of the loop, go left/west 0.2 miles, passing a junction for the Savanna Trail's larger loop; after that, go left/south onto Beaver Lodge Trail loop.

• **Hardwood Hills Trail** – Though this 1.1-mile loop trail through a forested area at the park's northern boundary heads off another cluster's trail, the Savanna Trail parking lot is the shortest route to it; you'll walk 4.1-miles round trip with the connecting trails. At the Wedge Hill Savanna Trail junction, go right/north, then at the Wetland Trail junction, head right/north; after passing below the railroad overpass, go right/

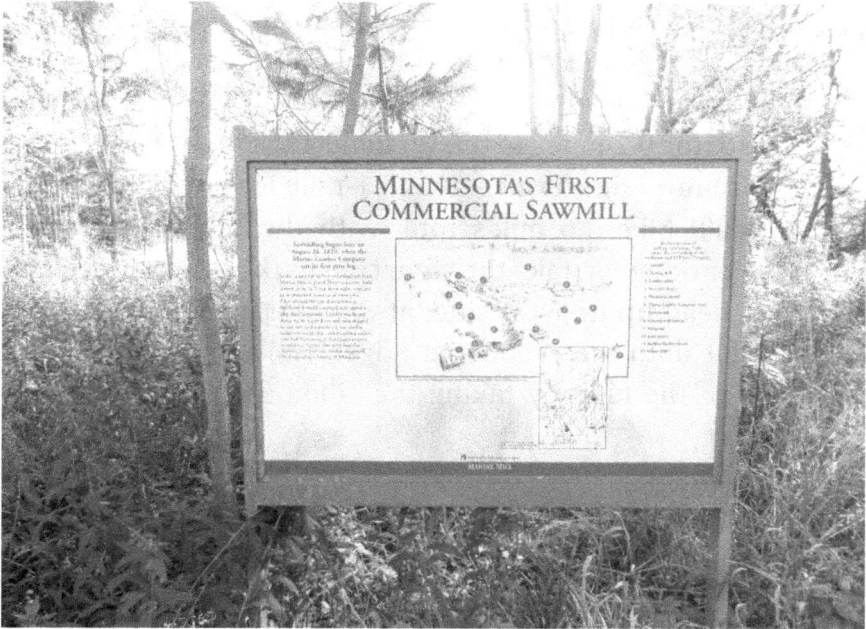

Sawmill and Waterfall Trail

northwest onto the Woodland Edge Trail. The next junction is the Hardwood Hills Trail.

• **Prairie Overlook Trail** – The 1.6-mile narrow loop with a pond at its center heads through both open country and a woods. From the parking lot, take the 0.1-mile stem trail to the loop.

• **Rolling Hills Savanna Trail** – This 1.1-mile loop gently rolls through a small woods; connecting trails make for a 4.1-mile round trip. Head up the Prairie Overlook Trail's west side. At the first junction, go left onto the Woodland Edge Trail and then take the next left/south onto the Rolling Hills Trail.

• **Wedge Hill Savanna Trail (small loop)** – This 0.5-mile loop sits on a prairie atop the river bluff. From the parking lot, take the connecting trail left/west to the Savanna Trail trailhead, going left at the first junction.

• **Wetland Trail** – The 2.2-mile loop heads around a blufftop wetlands; with connector trails, the hike runs about 2.6-miles round trip. At the trailhead for the Wedge Hill Savanna Trail, go right/north for 0.1 miles to the Wetland Trail loop.

• **Woodland Edge Trail** – This 2.1-mile loop runs through a forest; you'll hike 3.6 miles total with the connecting trails. From the parking lot, take the stem trail to the Prairie Overlook Trail and head up its west side; at the first junction, go either left or right onto the Woodland Edge Trail loop. You can add 1.1 miles to the loop by taking the adjoining Hardwood Hills Trail.

Polk County

Offering some of the most fantastic scenery on the St. Croix River, a trip north to Polk County is worth the drive for day hikers. Most notably near the St. Croix County border is a 25-foot waterfall and two rail lines heading through woodlands and pastoral farm scenes.

Cascade Falls Trail
St. Croix National Scenic Riverway

A 25-foot waterfall awaits hikers on a very short trail in the village of Osceola.

The Cascade Falls Trail runs less than a couple of hundred feet – and most of that is up and down a stairs from the street to the glen where the falls sits.

To reach the trailhead, take Wis. Hwy. 35 into Osceola. As entering downtown, the highway becomes North Cascade Street. Park anywhere downtown along the street.

Signs mark the trailhead, located on the street's east side across from First Avenue. To reach the trail, a steep staircase that looks like it was extracted from a fire tower heads from the sidewalk to Willkie Glen.

Majestic trees shade the staircase and glen in green. You'll be able to hear the waterfall's roar from the sidewalk – and easily spot it once you reach the glen.

Osceola Creek drops over the natural falls as it flows westward on its way to the St. Croix River. Between the village and the river, the creek descends 100 feet in altitude, but this

Cascade Falls

waterfalls is the only large drop.

The falls wouldn't exist if not for the river. At the end of the last ice age some 10,000 years ago, floodwaters from melting glaciers carved out a large gorge. The waterfall is a one of the vertical wall cuts in that gorge. It measures 30 feet across.

The village itself might not exist if not for the falls. Osceola was settled because the falls could support industry; in the late 1800s, it powered a mill.

The smaller and narrower Geiger Falls is upstream on Osceola Creek, but there's no hiking path between it and Cascade Falls.

The best time to hike the trail is in spring when snow melt increases the amount of water flowing over the falls. Another good time to visit: at night when the village lights up the falls using LED lighting to mimic the glow of the full moon upon the water; coloring is changed for the seasons.

A dirt footpath does lead from Cascade Falls to the St. Croix. The village has plans to improve the walkway into a more accessible trail.

In the centuries ahead, the waterfalls actually will be its own undoing – the splash of water at its base has created a kick-point in the vertical wall that is slowly eroding and undercutting the drop, which one day will causing it to collapse. The waterfalls then will become a cascades, or series of rock steps, that the creek flows over.

Stower Seven Lake State Trail
Amery-Osceola/Dresser

Peaceful woodland, serene ponds, and picturesque farms await day hikers on the Stower Seven Lakes State Trail heading west of Amery.

Built on a former rail line, the 14-mile trail heads to a mile short of Dresser. A good segment to take is from the trailhead in Amery for about 3 miles to the southern tip of Bear Trap Lake.

With a surface of crushed limestone and the generally level grade of rail lines – to save locomotive fuel consumption, railroads sought grades of no more than 3 percent for their lines – the trail is easy for families with children to handle. Milepost signs conveniently punctuate the trail.

In Amery, the trail begins on Harriman Avenue west of Wis. Hwy. 46. A public parking lot is near the trail just east of Harriman Avenue.

About 0.2 miles in as leaving Amery, the trail crosses between North Twin and South Twin lakes. On North Twin Lake, a popular fishing destination, watch for bald eagles diving to snare walleye or Northern pike for a meal. Loons also can be spotted here.

At just under a mile, the trail crosses Baker Avenue. Though the area is moderately built up, the trail is nicely wooded with

Stower Seven Lake State Trail

maple and oak, keeping you isolated from the sights of modern life.

Around 1.5 miles, the trail skirts a small group of ponds to the north. After that, farmland is visible between the tree breaks to the north and soon becomes more prevalent.

The trail is named for Harvey and Marilyn Stower of Amery. For many years, Harvey served in the Wisconsin Legislature and as Amery's mayor.

As nearing Deronda, the trail intersects a couple of highways, so be safe when crossing them. The first of them comes at about 2.5 miles, when the trail junctions with State Highway 115. The next comes at about 2.8 miles with County Road F.

About three miles in, the trail reaches the southern tip of Bear Trap Lake with Kinney Lake to the south. This marks a good spot to turn around.

If time and energy permits, though, continue onward. At Deronda, the trail heads three more miles to Wanderoos, then 5 miles to Nye, and finally 2.5 miles to its end at 90th Avenue near Dresser.

Osceola/Dresser trailhead – The trail begins east of Osceola at Lotus Lake. From there, you can walk about two miles along Horse Creek to Horse Lake for a 4-mile round trip.

Clear Lake-Clayton Trail

Eleven miles of old rail bed have been converted into a walking path running between the two Polk County villages of Clear Lake and Clayton, the trail's namesakes. The Wisconsin trail passes several lakes as it nears Clayton.

A good segment of the Clear Lake-Clayton Trail to hike during summer is a 3-mile round trip west of Clayton from County Road P to 65th Avenue.

Park at the public boat landing for Magnor Lake on U.S. Hwy. 63 west of Clayton. Magnor Lake covers 229 acres and at 26 feet deep is a popular spot for catching panfish, largemouth bass, Northern pike and walleye. The lake's water clarity is low, though.

To reach the trailhead, you'll have to cross Hwy. 63 as the trail is on the south/east of that road. Exercise caution as crossing and watch for traffic turning off of County Road P onto Hwy. 63.

The fairly flat and wide trail parallels Hwy. 63, but a good mix of hardwood trees and bushes line both sides of the path, keeping out the views of passing traffic and offering moderate shade. The trail is popular among ATVs, but there's plenty of room for both three-wheelers and walkers.

Heading south from Magnor Lake, you'll enter farm country with fields visible through the tree breaks on both sides of the trail.

Not quite half-way to your turnback point, you'll catch sight of and pass Barbo Lake, also on your right. Though a shallow lake at only four-feet deep, it covers 43.5 acres.

From there, the trail curves southward. Near the turnback point, you'll likely spot Paulson Lake between the trees on the right. At 25 acres and 12 feet deep, the lake sports panfish, largemouth bass and Northern pike.

Upon reaching 65th Avenue, you've gone 1.5 miles. This marks a good spot to head back.

Other Polk County Trails
Amery

• **Amery Regional Medical Center Walking Trail** – The local hospital grounds provides a community walking path running along the Apple River. The forested route nicely keeps views of the urban area to a minimum.

• **Green Trail** – North of the city, a trio of trails at the Balsam Branch Cross Country Ski Trails make their way through woodlands for hiking, skiing and snowshoeing. Try the Green

Trail, a 3-mile trail that includes a segment circling a pond with swans.

• **Cattail State Trail** – This route, located on what used to be old railroad tracks, runs for nearly 18 miles on an old Soo Line rail line between Amery and Almena. The Amery end begins in a woodlands then passes through farmland and prairie.

• **York Park Walking Trail** – Three miles of graveled trails take hikers through a hardwood forest and past a lakeshore in this 40-acre park. Despite the park's urban setting, it's a prime spot to spot a variety of birds, including common loons, bald eagles and osprey.

Clear Lake

• **Cattail State Trail** – North of town, pick up the state trail that runs between Amery and Almena. Crushed stone covers the route, and the old rail line is smooth with the most gradual of elevation gains.

• **Clear Lake Village Park** – A short trail takes hikers through tall oaks and white-barked birch trees to French Lake. In autumn, an array of colors from the variety of trees in the 260-acre park are impressive.

Osceola-Dresser

• **Ridgeview Trail** – Hikers can walk across billion-year-old lava flows in a 2.1-mile loop at Osceola Bedrock Glades State Natural Area. This area is one of only three bedrock glade ecosystems in the state.

• **Ridge View (Osceola and Chisago loops) Trail** – This pair of St. Croix National Scenic Riverway trails gives you great close-up views of a St. Croix River back channel. Birds abound in this secluded woodland.

• For more Polk County hikes, see this title's sister book, **Hittin' the Trail: Day Hiking Polk County**.

Dunn County

M ost of western Dunn County is farmland with steeper wooded areas set aside by their owners for private hunting. Still, a few good trails can be found that are worth venturing across the county line to hike.

Bjornson Education-Recreation Center Loop
Bjornson Education-Recreation Center

You can enjoy a pleasant walk through woodlands and past a small, spring-fed creek on a looping trail at the Bjornson Education-Recreation Center.

The 1.7-mile loop actually is a set of interconnecting trails at the 443-acre school forest owned by the School District of the Menomonie Area. A plethora of walking paths and logging trails, which double as cross country ski routes in winter, run through the recreation center.

Any day in summer and weekends during late spring and early autumn marks a good time to visit. Weekdays during the school year can be crowded and noisy as school kids may be on the site for classwork.

To reach the recreation center, from Interstate 94 west of Menomonie, take Exit 32 north on County Road Q. Turn right/east onto 700th Avenue then right/southwest onto 160th Avenue. As 160th Avenue curves sharply south, turn right/southwest onto the recreational center's main entrance road. Park off the entrance road in front of the gate. Do not drive past the gate, as you may get locked in.

Walk the entrance road into the center, passing a man-made pond along the way. During the 1970s, beavers constructed a natural pond upstream, but their overeagerness caused a great amount of flooding, forcing their removal; to compensate for the lost educational opportunity, the pond and wetlands alongside the entrance road were developed.

In about 0.4 miles, you'll reach the main group area, which includes a shelter, picnic tables, and pit toilets. On the group area's north side, you'll notice ruins for what used to be a barn and milk house as well as a side trail that leads to the foundation of an old farmhouse. Through the first half of the 20th century, the recreation center was a working, privately-owned farm.

From the group area, take the Spring Trail south. If standing at the group area's center and looking west, you'll notice one trail heads that direction; to its left a trail heads southwest, then to its left going straight south is the Spring Trail. The Spring Trail is largely a grassy, mowed area.

In about 0.2 miles, go on the trail heading directly west. You'll enter the recreation center's forested area. Bring along a tree guide and see if you identify the many northern hardwoods along the trail. Among them are ash, basswood, maple, oak, white birch, and yellow birch.

At the next junction, in about 0.07 miles, go right/north. Watch for the lean-tos built on the trail's right side. Every year, hundreds of elementary and middle school students visit the site to learn about nature, a tradition since the early 1970s when the school district purchased the forest from Ed Bjornson of the Spring Valley Lumber Company. Keep an eye out for lost mittens.

The trail loops back west. At the next junction, in about 0.25 miles, go right/north. You'll cross two bridges, the first of

which goes over a stream feeding Hay Creek and the second of which is Hay Creek. Several strong springs in the surrounding hillsides feed the waterway.

In about 0.07 miles, you'll reach the next junction, a logging road. Go right/east. Profits from timber sales at the school forest pay for the facility and environmental education in the district. Students also plant trees here and collect acorns for state tree nurseries.

The logging road runs past towering red pines and alongside the ever gurgling Hay Creek, then after about a third of a mile reaches the main group area. From there, follow the entrance road back to your vehicle.

Other Dunn County Trails

• **Bjornson Education-Recreation Center Back Trail** – A logging road heads down a hillside to a ravine created by an intermittent creek and connects with a trail heading to the center's main campus. Park in a gravel lot off of 700th Avenue east of County Road Q.

• **Gilbert Creek Trail** – Hikers can walk along bucolic Gilbert Creek, whose banks recently were restored. This is best hiked in spring or in autumn after a hard freeze when grass is low. A small gravel lot sits off of County Road N north of Wis. Hwy. 29.

• **Knapp School Hill Trail** – Generations of kids at the local elementary school used to sled down the school-owned hill during recess each winter. In the 1990s, though, trees were allowed to overtake the hill, but the trails up the sandstone rise remain. Park in the elementary school lot off of Main Street on weekends or during summer.

• **Bolen Creek State Public Hunting Trails** – Primitive trails cut through this small wooded area near Connorsville. Do not visit this area during hunting season. Park off of 1270th Street just west of County Road Q.

Pierce County

S Sharing St. Croix County's geology and geography, Pierce County offers several great day hikes that also explore riverways and peaceful woodlands. Among them are trails along the Kinnickinnic River and through Wisconsin's largest cave system.

Glen Park Trail
Glen Park, River Falls

A swinging bridge and a cascades that cuts through 500-million-year-old rock await day hikers on the Glen Park Trail in River Falls.

The 0.25-mile round trip set of trails – christened here after the park they run through – sits close to the University of Wisconsin-River Falls campus. Because of that, parking can be difficult to find, so a visit is best done during summer when the student population shrinks.

To reach the trailhead, head south from downtown River Falls on South Main Street. At West Cascade Street, turn right/west. Street parking is available between Main Street and Winter/State Street. The trailhead is west of Winter/State Street and heads southwest into a wooded area.

You'll immediately come to the Glen Park Swinging Bridge, a River Falls icon. A swinging bridge was constructed in 1925 and though a replica now stands there, parts of the original stonework marking the entrance remains.

As reaching the bridge's center, look over the side at the

Glen Park Trail

gorge below. You'll be able to hear and see part of the rapids. The South Fork of the Kinnickinnic River rumbles through sandstone that settled there some 500 million years ago when that part of the world was covered by a shallow, tropical sea.

The world looked much different then. With life limited to the sea, the coastline about 60 miles to the north would have been barren and hot with daytime temperatures often hitting 100 degrees F. Days were shorter, too, lasting only about 20 hours.

Upon crossing the swinging bridge, you've entered Glen Park, a favorite spot for local residents to picnic since the 1860s, and the city's oldest park. Take the trail right/north-west through a shaded area then downhill to the gorge's bottom. Once there, walk southeast toward the rapids.

The South Fork rushes north into the Kinnickinnic River, a

major trout stream in the region. Fishermen casting rods often can be spotted in the gorge, which at one time was considered a glen (hence the park's name).

When done looking about, return the way you came. You can extend the hike slightly by staying on the trail rather than turning back onto the swinging bridge. The park also contains a playground.

Purple Trail
Kinnickinnic State Park

Day hikers are certain to spot wildlife on the Purple Trail at the southernmost state park along the St. Croix River.

The 1.2-mile loop, which includes a segment of the Yellow Trail, takes hikers along a first-class trout stream.

To reach the trail, follow the entry road west all of the way to its end and park in the St. Croix Picnic Area Lot. An access trail to the main course begins in the lot's western corner.

Upon reaching the Purple Trail, turn right/north. Most of the trees in this area of Wisconsin were cut by pioneers and 19th century logging companies, but the trail here passes through one of the few woodlands to escape the ax.

Wildlife abounds as well in this area. Watch for whitetail deer, raccoons, rabbits and squirrels. Hikers have spotted weasels, gray fox, red fox and even beaver nearby.

In about 600 feet from the access trail, you'll pass a path to the swim area. Continuing on the main trail, the woods soon gives way to a restored prairie.

This region was plowed under by the area's first white settlers but since 1972 (when the state park was established) have been among 50 acres of land at the park restored to original prairie. Watch for partridge, ringneck pheasants and other birds that prefer grasslands.

Confluence of the Kinnickinnic and St. Croix rivers

You'll soon reach a junction with the Yellow Trail; go right/ south on it through more prairie. In about 600 feet, you'll cross the park entry road, so make sure any little ones with you watch for traffic.

The Yellow Trail then rejoins the Purple Trail; go right/ south onto the latter. After a junction with the Orange Trail, the Kinnickinnic River should come in view to the left/south. You're on a bluff overlooking the river; don't get too close to the edge, though, as the limestone cliff is a straight drop down.

White pines line the river, which is popular with anglers for its brown trout. Watch for mink slinking along the banks looking for food.

Rounding the picnic area, head into the overlook on the left/west to see the Kinnickinnic River Delta with the St. Croix River. Sediment from the Kinnickinnic reduces the St. Croix's width here by about 75 percent.

The result is a faster current, which during winter leaves it ice free. Because of that, bald eagles enjoy a year-round fishing area, so keep your eyes to the sky for the bird of prey.

The access trail to the parking lot is directly across from the overlook.

If time and energy allows, consider extending the hike by adding the rest of the Yellow Trail; to do that, at the first junction of the Purple/Yellow trails, go left/north onto the latter. The 1.2-mile Yellow Trail (You'll only do about a mile of it for a 1.8-mile hike total.) loops along the forest and prairie edge. A flat trail, it offers the opportunity to spot wild turkeys. When the Yellow rejoins the Purple, go left/south onto the latter.

Alternately, enjoy a dip into the St. Croix River at its swim area that the Purple Trail passed at its beginning. There's a small sand beach at the swim area, and the St. Croix is one of the state's cleanest waterways.

Crystal Cave Tour
Crystal Cave, Spring Valley

Day hikers can explore Wisconsin's longest cave near the village of Spring Valley.

The Crystal Cave tour runs about 0.5-miles round trip through 1,300 feet of passageways. Several deeper passages are closed to the public. The cave is a commercial venture, so a fee is charged to be part of a tour.

To reach Crystal Cave, from Spring Valley take Wis. Hwy. 29 west. In about a mile after ascending the hill, turn left/south onto the cave entrance road. After parking, go into the gift shop to purchase tour tickets.

In 1881, a teenage boy discovered the cave when pursuing a squirrel that disappeared down a sinkhole. The next day, he

Crystal Cave

and his brother returned and with rope and lantern explored a small portion of it. During the early 1940s, a businessman had the clay and rock debris removed from the sinkhole and opened the cave to the public for tours; it was named for the quartz crystals that appear throughout the cave's walls.

The cave runs through a chunk of dolomite, a type of limestone, that formed about 485 million years ago when this part of the world was a covered by a shallow sea; two fossils of nickel-sized snail-like creatures can be seen in cave's floor. It is seven stories deep and 4000 feet long.

Your tour leaves from the gift shop, descending down stairs through the sinkhole discovered in the 1880s. Ramps then pass man-made pools that cleverly control the water draining into the living cave.

In short order, the tour enters the Ballroom, the cave's

largest chamber. Following that, several passageways head past stalactites, stalagmites and rippling flowstone.

The cave is home to several bat species; both big and brown bats hibernate there in winter. Usually a bat or two can be spotted sleeping above you in a passageway.

Among the tour highlights is the Spook Room, where the tour guide turns off the lights to show just how dark the cave is. The darkness actually feels impenetrable.

From there, the tour heads to the Story Room, where a humorous story of Cave Man Charley is presented. Among the last stops is the Wish Room, whose walls are filled with coins; the rock walls contain a large amount of illite, a mineral used for a variety of disparate purposes, including cosmetics, dam repair, and medicine.

The cave remains a constant 50 degrees, so when visiting always wear a sweatshirt and pants, even on summer's hottest days. Crystal Cave generally is only open from April through mid-October with slightly longer hours in late spring through summer.

Other Pierce County Trails

Kinnickinnic State Park

Among the trails at the state park (going from east to west):

• **Red Trail** – The 1.6-mile hike heads through prairie alongside a forest's edge. Among the highlights is the Vulture's Peak area. Near the park entrance, the set of two loops can be accessed from the park's first two parking lot.

• **Blue Trail** – The 0.7-mile out-and-back trail (1.4-miles round trip) gives hikers the opportunity to explore gorges and coulees into the Kinnickinnic River Valley. Access the wooded trail from the second parking area past the park entrance. Add the 0.1-mile (0.2-miles round trip) Brown Trail, which serves as a sledding hill in winter, to extend the hike.

• **Yellow Trail** – The 1.2-mile loop edges a forest and prairie area. Watch for deer, pheasants and turkeys along the trail. The Kinni Overlook Lot is a good place to start; the trail can be extended by adding the Green, Orange or Purple trails.

• **Orange Trail** – A wooded out-and-back trail atop the Kinnickinnic River bluffs, it runs for 0.5 miles (1-mile round trip). Park at the Kinni Overlook Lot and access it via the Yellow Trail; add the Purple and Yellow trails for a longer walk.

• **Green Trail** – The trail loops about the outside of a prairie area under restoration and is an excellent place to spot partridge, pheasants and other birds. Access it via the Yellow Trail; from the Kinnic Overlook Lot, go left/north on the Yellow for a 1.6-mile round trip (The Green Trail itself is 1.1-miles long).

River Falls

• **Manion Wildlife Area walkabout** – If you enjoy bushwhacking or primitive trails, try this 158-acre property that includes restored grasslands. A parking lot sits on the south side of County Road FF east of 1130th Street,

• **Jackson Preserve walkabout** – Ditto for the adjacent Jackson Preserve, a 46-acre Kinnickinnic River Land Trust property on the north side of County FF. Use the wildlife area's parking lot.

Spring Valley

• **Sinkhole Nature Trail** – The free half-mile trail on the Crystal Cave property passes two sinkholes, gooseberry brambles, and mossy banks. The trailhead is immediately north of the parking lot.

• **Wildwood Trail** – Among the most accessible and pleasurable parts of the trail runs 1.7 miles round-trip from near downtown alongside a small stream through a comely woods. The trailhead is off of Herb Avenue, north of County Road B (N. Second St.).

Best Trails Lists

W hich trails are the best for watching birds? Strolling on a beach? Enjoying a waterfall? Here are some lists of the best St. Croix County trails for those and many other specific interests.

Beaches
- Beach Trail
- Hudson Pier
- Glen Hills West Trail

Birdwatching
- Trout Brook (Purple) Trail
- Parnell Prairie Reserve loops
- Casey Lake Trail

Campgrounds
- Pioneer (Yellow) Trail
- Willow Falls (Blue) Trail
- Glen Hills East Trail

Geology
- Willow Falls (Gray) Trail
- Willow Falls (Blue) Trail
- Crystal Cave (Pierce County)

History/Archeology
- Paperjack Creek and Heritage Center Trails

- Wildwood Trail
- Boom Site Trail (Washington County)

Must-do's
- Willow Falls Hill (Gray) Trail
- Paperjack Creek and Heritage Center Trails
- Eau Galle Dam Trail

Picnicking
- Mary Park Trail
- North River Trail (Washington County)
- Purple Trail (Pierce County)

Plant communities
- Parnell Prairie Reserve Trail
- Knapweed (Orange) Trail
- Cylon State Wildlife Area Trail

Primitive trails/Bushwhacking
- Kelly Creek Preserve Trail
- Kinnickinnic Headwaters Trail
- Cylon State Wildlife Area Trail

Vistas
- Glen Hills East Trail
- Pioneer (Yellow) Trail
- Eau Galle Dam Trail

Waterfalls
- Willow Falls Hill (Gray) Trail
- Glen Park Trail (Pierce County)
- Fairy Falls (Washington County)

• Cascade Falls Trail (Polk County)

Wheelchair accessible
• Hidden Ponds (Black) Nature Trail
• Riverside Trail (Washington County)

Wildflowers
• Hidden Ponds (Black) Nature Trail
• Cylon State Wildlife Area Trail
• Kelly Creek Preserve Trail

Wildlife
• Casey Lake Trail
• Glen Hills East Trail
• Purple Trail (Pierce County)

Bonus Section:
Day Hiking Primer

Y ou'll get more out of a day hike if you research it and plan ahead. It's not enough to just pull over to the side of the road and hit a trail that you've never been on and have no idea where it goes. In fact, doing so invites disaster.

Instead, you should preselect a trail (This book's trail descriptions can help you do that). You'll also want to ensure that you have the proper clothing, equipment, navigational tools, first-aid kit, food and water. Knowing the rules of the trail and potential dangers along the way also are helpful. In this special section, we'll look at each of these topics to ensure you're fully prepared.

Selecting a Trail

For your first few hikes, stick to short, well-known trails where you're likely to encounter others. Once you get a feel for hiking, your abilities, and your interests, expand to longer and more remote trails.

Always check to see what the weather will be like on the trail you plan to hike. While an adult might be able to withstand wind and a sprinkle here or there, for kids it can be pure misery. Dry, pleasantly warm days with limited wind always are best when hiking with children.

Don't choose a trail that is any longer than the least fit person in your group can hike. Adults in good shape can go 8-

12 miles a day; for kids, it's much less. There's no magical number.

When planning the hike, try to find a trail with a mid-point payoff – that is something you and definitely any children will find exciting about half-way through the hike. This will help keep up everyone's energy and enthusiasm during the journey.

If you have children in your hiking party, consider a couple of additional points when selecting a trail.

Until children enter their late teens, they need to stick to trails rather than going off-trail hiking, which is known as bushwhacking. Children too easily can get lost when off trail. They also can easily get scratched and cut up or stumble across poisonous plants and dangerous animals.

Generally, kids will prefer a circular route to one that requires hiking back the way you came. The return trip often feels anti-climatic, but you can overcome that by mentioning features that all of you might want to take a closer look at.

Once you select a trail, it's time to plan for your day hike. Doing so will save you a lot of grief – and potentially prevent an emergency. You are, after all, entering the wilds, a place where help may not be readily available.

When planning your hike, follow these steps:

• Print a road map showing how to reach the parking lot near the trailhead. Outline the route with a transparent yellow highlighter and write out the directions.

• Print a satellite photo of the parking area and the trailhead. Mark the trailhead on the photo.

• Print a topo map of the trail. Outline the trail with the yellow highlighter. Note interesting features you want to see along the trail and the destination.

• If carrying GPS, program this information into your device.

• Make a timeline for your trip, listing: when you will leave home; when you will arrive at the trailhead; your turn back time; when you will return for home in your vehicle; and when you will arrive at your home.

• Estimate how much water and food you will need to bring based on the amount of time you plan to spend on the trail and in your vehicle. You'll need at least two pints of water per person for every hour on the trail.

• Fill out two copies of a hiker's safety form. Leave one in your vehicle.

• Share all of this information with a responsible person remaining in civilization, leaving a hiker's safety form with them. If they do not hear from you within an hour of when you plan to leave the trail in your vehicle, they should contact authorities to report you as possibly lost.

Clothing

Footwear

If your feet hurt, the hike is over, so getting the right footwear is worth the time. Making sure the footwear fits before hitting the trail also is a good idea. With children, if you've gone a few weeks without hiking, that's plenty of time for feet to grow, and they may have just outgrown their hiking boots. Check out everyone's footwear a few days before head-ing out on the hike. If it doesn't fit, replace it.

For flat, smooth, dry trails, sneakers and cross-trainers are fine, but if you really want to head onto less traveled roads or tackle areas that aren't typically dry, you'll need hiking boots. Once you start doing any rocky or steep trails – and remember that a trail you consider moderately steep needs to be only half that angle for a child to consider it extremely steep – you'll want hiking boots, which offer rugged tread perfect for hand-ling rough trails.

Socks

Socks serve two purposes: to wick sweat away from skin and to provide cushioning. Cotton socks aren't very good for hiking, except in extremely dry environments, because they retain moisture that can lead to blisters. Wool socks or liner socks work best. You'll want to look for three-season socks, also known as trekking socks. While a little thicker than summer socks, their extra cushioning generally prevents blisters. Also, make sure kids don't put on holey socks; that's just inviting blisters.

Layering

On all but hot, dry days, when hiking you should wear multiple layers of clothing that provide various levels of protection against sweat, heat loss, wind and potentially rain. Layering works because the type of clothing you select for each stratum serves a different function, such as wicking moisture or shielding against wind. In addition, trapped air between each layer of clothing is warmed by your body heat. Layers also can be added or taken off as needed.

Generally, you need three layers. Closest to your skin is the wicking layer, which pulls perspiration away from the body and into the next layer, where it evaporates. Exertion from walking means you will sweat and generate heat, even if the weather is cold. The second layer provides insulation, which helps keep you warm. The last layer is a water-resistant shell that protects you from rain, wind, snow and sleet.

As the seasons and weather change, so does the type of clothing you select for each layer. The first layer ought to be a loose-fitting T-shirt in summer, but in winter and on other cold days you might opt for a long-sleeved moisture-wicking synthetic material, like polypropylene. During winter, the next layer probably also should cover the neck, which often is exposed to the elements. A turtleneck works fine, but preferably not one made of cotton. The third layer in winter, depending on the temperature, could be a wool sweater, a half-zippered long sleeved fleece jacket, or a fleece vest.

You might even add a fourth layer of a hooded parka with pockets, made of material that can block wind and resist water. Gloves or mittens as well as a hat also are necessary on cold days.

Headgear

Half of all body heat is lost through the head, hence the hiker's adage, "If your hands are cold, wear a hat." In cool, wet weather, wearing a hat is at least good for avoiding hypothermia, a potentially deadly condition in which heat loss occurs faster than the body can generate it. Children are more susceptible to hypothermia than adults.

Especially during summer, a hat with a wide brim is useful in keeping the sun out of eyes. It's also nice should rain start falling.

For young children, get a hat with a chin strap. They like to play with their hats, which will fly off in a wind gust if not fastened some way to the child.

Sunglasses

Sunglasses are an absolute must if walking through open areas exposed to the sun and in winter when you can suffer from snow blindness. Look for 100% UV-protective shades, which provide the best screen.

Equipment

A couple of principles should guide your purchases. First,

the longer and more complex the hike, the more equipment you'll need. Secondly, your general goal is to go light. Since you're on a day hike, the amount of gear you'll need is a fraction of what backpackers shown in magazines and catalogues usually carry. Still, the inclination of most day hikers is to not carry enough equipment. For the lightness issue, most gear today is made with titanium and siliconized nylon, ensuring it is sturdy yet fairly light. While the following list of what you need may look long, it won't weigh much.

Backpacks

Sometimes called daypacks (for day hikes or for kids), backpacks are essential to carry all of the essentials you need – snacks, first-aid kit, extra clothing.

For day hiking, you'll want to get yourself an internal frame, in which the frame giving the backpack its shape is inside the pack's fabric so it's not exposed to nature. Such frames usually are lightweight and comfortable. External frames have the frame outside the pack, so they are exposed to the elements. They are excellent for long hikes into the backcountry when you must carry heavy loads.

As kids get older, and especially after they've been hiking for a couple of years, they'll want a "real" backpack. Unfortunately, most backpacks for kids are overbuilt and too heavy. Even light ones that safely can hold up to 50 pounds are inane for most children.

When buying a daypack for your child, look for sternum straps, which help keep the strap on the shoulders. This is vital for prepubescent children, as they do not have the broad shoulders that come with adolescence, meaning packs likely will slip off and onto their arms, making them uncomfortable and difficult to carry. Don't buy a backpack that a child will "grow into." Backpacks that don't fit well simply will lead to sore shoulder and back muscles and could result in poor posture.

Also, consider purchasing a daypack with a hydration system for kids. This will help ensure they drink a lot of water. More on this later when we get to canteens.

Before hitting the trail, always check your children's backpacks to make sure that they have not overloaded them. Kids think they need more than they really do. They also tend to overestimate their own ability to carry stuff. Sibling rivalries often lead to children packing more than they should in their rucksacks, too. Don't let them overpack "to teach them a lesson," though, as it can damage bones and turn the hike into a bad experience.

A good rule of thumb is no more than 25 percent capacity. Most upper elementary school kids can carry only about 10 pounds for any short distance. Subtract the weight of the backpack, and that means only 4-5 pounds in the backpack. Overweight children will need to carry a little less than this or they'll quickly be out of breath.

Child carriers

You'll have to carry infant and toddlers. Until infants can hold their heads up, which usually doesn't happen until about four to six months of age, a front pack (like a Snugli or Baby Bjorn) is best. It keeps the infant close for warmth and balances out your backpack. At the same time, though, you must watch for baby overheating in a front pack, so you'll need to remove the infant from your body at rest stops.

Once children reach about 20 pounds, they typically can hold their heads up and sit on their own. At that point, you'll want a baby carrier (sometimes called a child carrier or baby backpack), which can transfer the infant's weight to your hips when you walk. You'll not only be comfortable, but your child will love it, too.

Look for a baby carrier that is sturdy yet lightweight. Your child is going to get heavier as time passes, so about the only way you can counteract this is to reduce the weight of the items you use to carry things. The carrier also should have adjustment points, as you don't want your child to outgrow the carrier too soon. A padded waist belt and padded shoulder straps are necessary for your comfort. The carrier should provide some kind of head and neck support if you're hauling an infant. It also should offer back support for children of all ages, and leg holes should be wide enough so there's no chafing. You want to be able to load your infant without help, so it should be stable enough to stand that way when you take it off the child can sit in it for a moment while you get turned around. Stay away from baby carriers with only shoulder straps as you need the waist belt to help shift the child's weight to your hips for more comfortable walking.

Fanny packs

Also known as a belt bag, a fanny pack is virtually a must for anyone with a baby carrier, as you can't otherwise lug a backpack. If your significant other is with you, he or she can carry the backpack, of course. Still, the fanny pack also is a good alternative to a backpack in hot weather, as it will reduce back sweat.

If you have only one or two kids on a hike, or if they also are old enough to carry daypacks, your fanny pack need not be large. A mid-size pouch can carry at least 200 cubic inches of supplies, which is more than enough to accommodate all the materials you need. A good fanny pack also has a spot for hooking canteens to.

Canteens

Canteens or plastic bottles filled with water are vital for any hike, no matter how short the trail. You'll need to have enough of them to carry about two pints of water per person for every hour of hiking.

Trekking poles

Also known as walking poles or walking sticks, trekking poles are necessary for maintaining stability on uneven or wet surfaces and to help reduce fatigue. The latter makes them useful on even surfaces. By transferring weight to the arms, a trekking pole can reduce stress on your knees and lower back, allowing you to maintain a better posture and to go farther.

If an adult with a baby or toddler on your back, you'll primarily want a trekking pole to help you maintain your balance, even if on a flat surface, and to help absorb some of the impact of your step.

Graphite tips provide the best traction. A basket just above the tip is a good idea so the stick doesn't sink into mud or sand. Angled cork handles are ergonomic and help absorb sweat from your hands so they don't blister. A strap on the handle to wrap around your hand is useful so the stick doesn't slip out. Telescopic poles are a good idea as you can adjust them as needed based on the terrain you're hiking and as kids grow to accommodate their height.

The pole also needs to be sturdy enough to handle rugged terrain, as you don't want a pole that bends when you press it to the ground. Spring-loaded shock absorbers help when heading down a steep incline but aren't necessary. Indeed, for a short walk across flat terrain, the right length stick is about all you need.

Carabiners

Carabiners are metal loops, vaguely shaped like a D, with a sprung or screwed gate. You'll find that hooking a couple of them to your backpack or fanny pack useful in many ways. For example, if you need to dig through a fanny pack, you can hook the strap of your trekking pole to it. Your hat, camera straps, first-aid kit, and a number of other objects also can connect to them. Hook carabiners to your fanny pack or backpack upon purchasing them so you don't forget them when packing. Small carabiners with sprung gates are inexpensive, but they do have a limited life span of a couple of dozen hikes.

Navigational Tools

Paper maps

Paper maps may sound passé in this age of GPS, but you'll find the variety and breadth of view they offer to be useful. During the planning process, a paper map (even if viewing it online), will be far superior to a GPS device. On the hike, you'll also want a backup to GPS. Or like many casual hikers, you may not own GPS at all, which makes paper maps indispensable.

Standard road maps (which includes printed guides and handmade trail maps) show highways and locations of cities and parks. Maps included in guidebooks, printed guides handed out at parks, and those that are hand-drawn tend to be designed like road maps, and often carry the same positives and negatives.

Topographical maps give contour lines and other important details for crossing a landscape. You'll find them invaluable on a hike into the wilds. The contour lines' shape and their spacing on a topo map show the form and steepness of a hill or bluff, unlike the standard road map and most brochures and hand-drawn trail maps. You'll also know if you're in a woods, which is marked in green, or in a clearing, which is marked in white. If you get lost, figuring out where you are and how to get to where you need to be will be much easier with such information.

Aerial photos offer a view from above that is rendered exactly as it would look from an airplane. Thanks to Google and other online services, you can get fairly detailed pictures of the landscape. Such pictures are an excellent resource when researching a hiking trail. Unfortunately, those pictures don't label what a feature is or what it's called, as would a topo map. Unless there's a stream, determining if a feature is a valley bottom or a ridgeline also can be difficult. Like topo maps, satellite and aerial photos can be out of date a few years.

GPS

By using satellites, the global positioning system can find your spot on the Earth to within 10 feet. With a GPS device, you can preprogram the trailhead location and mark key turns and landmarks as well as the hike's end point. This mobile map is a powerful technological tool that almost certainly ensures you won't get lost – so long as you've correctly programmed the information. GPS also can calculate travel time and act as a compass, a barometer and altimeter, making such devices virtually obsolete on a hike.

In remote areas, however, reception is spotty at best for GPS, rendering your mobile map worthless. A GPS device also runs on batteries, and there's always a chance they will go dead. Or you may drop your device, breaking it in the process. Their screens are small, and sometimes you need a large paper map to get a good sense of the natural landmarks around you.

Compass
Like a paper map, a compass is indispensable even if you use GPS. Should your GPS no longer function, the compass then can be used to tell you which direction you're heading. A protractor compass is best for hiking. Beneath the compass needle is a transparent base with lines to help your orient yourself. The compass often serves as a magnifying glass to help you make out map details. Most protractor compasses also come with a lanyard for easy carrying.

Food and Water
Water
As water is the heaviest item you'll probably carry, there is a temptation to not take as much as one should. Don't skimp on the amount of water you bring, though; after all, it's the one supply your body most needs. It's always better to end up having more water than needed than returning to your vehicle dehydrated.

How much water should you take? Adults need at least a quart for every two hours hiking. Children need to drink about a quart every two hours of walking and more if the weather is hot or dry. To keep kids hydrated, have them drink at every rest stop.

Don't presume there will be water on the hiking trail. Most trails outside of urban areas lack such an amenity. In addition, don't drink water from local streams, lakes, rivers or ponds. There's no way to tell if local water is safe or not. As soon as you have consumed half of your water supply, you should turn around for the vehicle.

Food
Among the many wonderful things about hiking is that

snacking between meals isn't frowned upon. Unless going on an all-day hike in which you'll picnic along the way, you want to keep everyone in your hiking party fed, especially as hunger can lead to lethargic and discontented children. It'll also keep young kids from snacking on the local flora or dirt. Before hitting the trail, you'll want to repackage as much of the food as possible as products sold at grocery stores tend to come in bulky packages that take up space and add a little weight to your backpack. Place the food in re-sealable plastic bags.

Bring a variety of small snacks for rest stops. You don't want kids filling up on snacks, but you do need them to maintain their energy levels if they're walking or to ensure they don't turn fussy if riding in a child carrier. Go for complex carbo-hy-drates and proteins for maintaining energy. Good options in-clude dried fruits, jerky, nuts, peanut butter, prepared energy bars, candy bars with a high protein content (nuts, peanut but-ter), crackers, raisins and trail mix (called "gorp"). A num-ber of trail mix recipes are available online; you and your child-ren may want to try them out at home to see which ones you col-lectively like most.

Salty treats rehydrate better than sweet treats do. Chocolate and other sweets are fine if they're not all that's served, but remember they also tend to lead to thirst and to make sticky messes. Whichever snacks you choose, don't experiment with food on the trail. Bring what you know kids will like.

Give the first snack within a half-hour of leaving the trailhead or you risk children becoming tired and whiny from low energy levels. If kids start asking for them every few steps even after having something to eat at the last rest stop, consider timing snacks to reaching a seeable landmark, such as, "We'll get out the trail mix when we reach that bend up ahead."

Milk for infants

If you have an infant or unweaned toddler with you, milk is as necessary as water. Children who only drink breastfed milk but don't have their mother on the hike require that you have breast-pumped milk in an insulated beverage container (such as a Thermos) that can keep it cool to avoid spoiling. Know how much the child drinks and at what frequency so you can bring enough. You'll also need to carry the child's bottle and feeding nipples. Bring enough extra water in your canteen so you can wash out the bottle after each feeding. A handkerchief can be used to dry bottles between feedings.

Don't forget the baby's pacifier. Make sure it has a string and hook attached so it connects to the baby's outfit and isn't lost.

What not to bring

Avoid soda and other caffeinated beverages, alcohol, and energy pills. The caffeine will dehydrate children as well as you. Alcohol has no place on the trail; you need your full faculties when making decisions and driving home. Energy pills essentially are a stimulant and like alcohol can lead to bad calls. If you're tired, get some sleep and hit the trail another day.

First-aid Kit

After water, this is the most essential item you can carry.

A first-aid kit should include:
- Adhesive bandages of various types and sizes, especially butterfly bandages (for younger kids, make sure they're colorful kid bandages)
- Aloe vera
- Anesthetic (such as Benzocaine)
- Antacid (tablets)

- Antibacterial (aka antibiotic) ointment (such as Neosporin or Bacitracin)
- Anti-diarrheal tablets (for adults only, as giving this to a child is controversial)
- Anti-itch cream or calamine lotion
- Antiseptics (such as hydrogen peroxide, iodine or Betadine, Mercuroclear, rubbing alcohol)
- Baking soda
- Breakable (or instant) ice packs
- Cotton swabs
- Disposable syringe (w/o needle)
- Epipen (if children or adults have allergies)
- Fingernail clippers (your multi-purpose tool might have this, and if so you can dispense with it)
- Gauze bandage
- Gauze compress pads (2x2 individually wrapped pad)
- Hand sanitizer (use this in place of soap)
- Liquid antihistamine (not Benadryl tablets, however, as children should take liquid not pills; be aware that liquid antihistamines may cause drowsiness)
- Medical tape
- Moisturizer containing an anti-inflammatory
- Mole skin
- Pain reliever (aka aspirin; for children's pain relief, use liquid acetaminophen such Tylenol or liquid ibuprofen; never give aspirin to a child under 12)
- Poison ivy cream (for treatment)
- Poison ivy soap
- Powdered sports drinks mix or electrolyte additives
- Sling
- Snakebite kit
- Thermometer

- Tweezers (your multi-purpose tool may have this allowing you to dispense with it)
- Water purification tablets

If infants are with you, be sure to also carry teething ointment (such as Orajel) and diaper rash treatment.

Many of the items should be taken out of their store packaging to make placement in your fanny pack or backpack easier. In addition, small amounts of some items – such as baking soda and cotton swabs – can be placed inside re-sealable plastic bags, since you won't need the whole amount purchased.

Make sure the first-aid items are in a waterproof container. A re-sealable plastic zipper bag is perfectly fine. As St. Croix County sports a humid climate, be sure to replace the adhesive bandages every couple of months, as they can deteriorate in the moistness. Also, check your first-aid kit every few trips and after any hike in which you've just used it, so that you can replace used components and to make sure medicines haven't expired.

If you have older elementary-age kids and teenagers who've been trained in first aid, giving them a kit to carry as well as yourself is a good idea. Should they find themselves lost or if you cannot get to them for a few moments, the kids might need to provide very basic first aid to one another.

Hiking with Children: Attitude Adjustment

To enjoy hiking with kids, you'll first have to adopt your child's perspective. Simply put, we must learn to hike on our kids' schedules – even though they may not know that's what we're doing.

Compared to adults, kids can't walk as far, they can't walk as fast, and they will grow bored more quickly. Every step we take requires three for them. In addition, early walkers, up to two years of age, prefer to wander than to "hike." Preschool kids will start to walk the trail, but at a rate of only about a mile per hour. With stops, that can turn a three-mile hike into a four-hour journey. Kids also won't be able to hike as steep of trails as you or handle as inclement of weather as you might.

This all may sound limiting, especially to long-time backpackers used to racking up miles or bagging peaks on their hikes, but it's really not. While you may have to put off some backcountry and mountain climbing trips for a while, it also opens to you a number of great short trails and nature hikes with spectacular sights that you may have otherwise skipped because they weren't challenging enough.

So sure, you'll have to make some compromises, but the payout is high. You're not personally on the hike to get a workout but to spend quality time with your children.

Family Dog

Dogs are part of the family, and if you have children, they'll want to share the hiking experience with their pets. In turn, dogs will have a blast on the trail, some larger dogs can be used as Sherpas, and others will defend against threatening animals.

But there is a downside to dogs. Many will chase animals and so run the risk of getting lost or injured. Also, a doggy bag will have to be carried for dog pooh – yeah, it's natural, but also inconsiderate to leave for other hikers to smell and for their kids to step in. In addition, most dogs almost always will lose a battle against a threatening animal, so there's a price to be paid for your safety.

Many places where you'll hike solve the dilemma for you as dogs aren't allowed on their trails. Dogs are verboten on some Wisconsin state parks trails but usually permitted on those in

116   ROB BIGNELL

national forests. Always check with the park ranger before heading to the trail.

If you can bring a dog, make sure it is well behaved and friendly to others. You don't need your dog biting another hiker while unnecessarily defending the family.

Rules of the Trail

Ah, the woods or a wide open meadow, peaceful and quiet, not a single soul around for miles. Now you and your children can do whatever you want.

Not so fast.

Act like wild animals on a hike, and you'll destroy the very aspects of the wilds that make them so attractive. You're also likely to end up back in civilization, specifically an emergency room. And there are other people around. Just as you would wish them to treat you courteously, so you and your children should do the same for them.

Let's cover how to act civilized on the trail.

Minimize damage to your surroundings

When on the trail, follow the maxim of "Leave no trace." Obviously, you shouldn't toss litter on the ground, start rockslides, or pollute water supplies. How much is damage and how much is good-natured exploring is a gray area, of course. Most serious backpackers will say you should never pick up objects, break branches, throw rocks, pick flowers, and so on – the idea is not to disturb the environment at all.

Good luck getting a four-year-old to think like that. The good news is a four-year-old won't be able to throw around many rocks or break most branches.

Still, children from their first hike into the wilderness should be taught to respect nature and to not destroy their environment. While you might overlook a preschooler hurling rocks into a puddle, they can be taught to sniff rather than pick flowers. As they grow older, you can teach them the value of leaving the rock alone. Regardless of age, don't allow children to write on boulders or carve into trees.

Many hikers split over picking berries. To strictly abide by the "minimize damage" principle, you wouldn't pick any berries at all. Kids, however, are likely to find great pleasure in eating blackberries, currants and thimbleberries as ambling down the trail. Personally, I don't see any problem enjoying a few berries if the long-term payoff is a respect and love for nature. To minimize damage, teach them to only pick berries they can reach from the trail so they don't trample plants or deplete food supplies for animals. They also should only pick what they'll eat.

Collecting is another issue. In national and most state and county parks, taking rocks, flower blossoms and even pine cones is illegal. Picking flowers moves many species, especially if they are rare and native, one step closer to extinction. Archeological ruins are extremely fragile, and even touching them can damage a site.

But on many trails, especially gem trails, collecting is part of the adventure. Use common sense – if the point of the trail is to find materials to collect, such as a gem trail, take judiciously, meaning don't overcollect. Otherwise, leave it there.

Sometimes the trail crosses private land. If so, walking around fields, not through them, always is best or you could damage a farmer's crops.

Pack out what you pack in

Set the example as a parent: Don't litter yourself; whenever stopping, pick up whatever you've dropped; and always require kids to pick up after themselves when they litter. In the spirit of "Leave no trace," try to leave the trail cleaner than you found it, so if you come across litter that's safe to pick up, do so and bring it back to a trash bin in civilization. Given this, you may want to bring a plastic bag to carry out garbage.

Picking up litter doesn't just mean gum and candy wrappers but also some organic materials that take a long time to decompose and aren't likely to be part of the natural environment you're hiking. In particular, these include peanut shells, orange peelings, and eggshells.

Burying litter, by the way, isn't viable. Either animals or erosion soon will dig it up, leaving it scattered around the trail and woods.

Stay on the trail

Hiking off trail means potentially damaging fragile growth. Following this rule not only ensures you minimize damage but is also a matter of safety. Off trail is where kids most likely will encounter dangerous animals and poisonous plants. Not being able to see where they're stepping also increases the likelihood of falling and injuring themselves. Leaving the trail raises the chances of getting lost. Staying on the trail also means staying out of caves, mines or abandoned structures you may encounter. They are usually dangerous places.

Finally, never let children take a shortcut on a switchback trail. Besides putting them on steep ground upon which they could slip, their impatient act causes the switchback to erode.

Trail Dangers

On St. Croix County trails, two common dangers face hikers: ticks and poison ivy/sumac. Both can make miserable your time on the trail or once back home. Fortunately, both threats are easily avoidable and treatable.

Ticks

One of the greatest dangers comes from the smallest of creatures: ticks. Both the wood and the deer tick are common in St. Croix County and can infect people with Lyme disease.

Ticks usually leap onto people from the top of a grass blade as you brush against it, so walking in the middle of the trail away from high plants is a good idea. Wearing a hat, a long sleeve shirt tucked into pants, and pants tucked into shoes or socks, also will keep ticks off you, though this is not foolproof as they sometimes can hook onto clothing. A tightly woven cloth provides the best protection, however. Children can pick up a tick that has hitchhiked onto the family dog, so outfit Rover and Queenie with a tick-repelling collar.

After hiking into an area where ticks live, you'll want to examine your children's bodies (as well as your own) for them. Check warm, moist areas of the skin, such as under the arms, the groin and head hair. Wearing light-colored clothing helps make the tiny tick easier to spot.

To get rid of a tick that has bitten your child, drip either disinfectant or rubbing alcohol on the bug, so it will loosen its grip. Grip the tick close to its head, slowly pulling it away from the skin. This hopefully will prevent it from releasing saliva that spreads disease. Rather than kill the tick, keep it in a plastic bag so that medical professionals can analyze it should disease symptoms appear. Next, wash the bite area with soap and water then apply antiseptic.

In the days after leaving the woods, also check for signs of disease from ticks. Look for bulls-eye rings, a sign of a Lyme disease. Other symptoms include a large red rash, joint pain, and flu-like symptoms. Indications of Rocky Mountain spotted fever include headache, fever, severe muscle aches, and a spotty rash first on palms and feet soles that spread, all beginning about two days after the bite.

If any of these symptoms appear, seek medical attention immediately. Fortunately, antibiotics exist to cure most tick-related diseases.

Poison ivy/sumac

Often the greatest danger in the wilds isn't our own clumsiness or foolhardiness but various plants we encounter. The good news is that we mostly have to force the encounter with flora. Touching the leaves of either poison ivy or poison sumac in particular results in an itchy, painful rash. Each plant's sticky resin, which causes the reaction, clings to clothing and hair, so you may not have "touched" a leaf, but once your hand runs against the resin on shirt or jeans, you'll probably get the rash.

To avoid touching these plants, you'll need to be able to identify each one. Remember the "Leaves of three, let it be" rule for poison ivy. Besides groups of three leaflets, poison ivy has shiny green leaves that are red in spring and fall. Poison sumac's leaves are not toothed as are non-poisonous sumac, and in autumn their leaves turn scarlet. Be forewarned that even after leaves fall off, poison oak's stems can carry some of the itchy resin.

By staying on the trail and walking down its middle rather than the edges, you are unlikely to come into contact with this pair of irritating plants. That probably is the best preventative. Poison ivy barrier creams also can be helpful, but they only temporarily block the resin. This lulls you into a false sense of safety, and so you may not bother to watch for poison ivy.

To treat poison ivy/sumac, wash the part of the body that

has touched the plant with poison ivy soap and cold water. This will erode the oily resin, so it'll be easier to rinse off. If you don't have any of this special soap, plain soap sometimes will work if used within a half-hour of touching the plant. Apply a poison ivy cream and get medical attention immediately. Wearing gloves, remove any clothing (including shoes) that has touched the plants, washing them and the worn gloves right away.

For more about these topics and many others, pick up this author's "Hikes with Tykes: A Practical Guide to Day Hiking with Kids." You also can find tips online at the author's "Day Hiking Trails" blog (*hikeswithtykes.blogspot.com*). Have fun on the trail!

About the Author

Rob Bignell is a long-time hiker, editor, and author of the popular "Best Sights to See," "Hikes with Tykes," "Headin' to the Cabin," and "Hittin' the Trail" guidebooks and several other titles. He and his son Kieran have been hiking together for the past decade. Rob has served as an infantryman in the Army National Guard and taught middle school students in New Mexico and Wisconsin. His newspaper work has won several national and state journalism awards, from editorial writing to sports reporting. In 2001, *The Prescott Journal*, which he served as managing editor of, was named Wisconsin's Weekly Newspaper of the Year. Rob and Kieran live in Wisconsin.

CHECK OUT THESE OTHER HIKING BOOKS BY ROB BIGNELL

"Best Sights to See" series:
• America's National Parks
• Great Smoky Mountain National Park
• Rocky Mountain National Park
• Voyageurs National Park

"Hikes with Tykes" series:
• Hikes with Tykes: A Practical Guide to Day Hiking
  with Children
• Hikes with Tykes: Games and Activities

"Headin' to the Cabin" series:
• Day Hiking Trails of Northeast Minnesota
• Day Hiking Trails of Northwest Wisconsin

"Hittin' the Trail" series:
National parks
• Grand Canyon National Park (ebook only)
Minnesota
• Gooseberry Falls State Park
• Split Rock Lighthouse State Park
Minnesota/Wisconsin
• Interstate State Park
• St. Croix National Scenic Riverway
Wisconsin
• Barron County
• Bayfield County

- Burnett County (ebook only)
- Chippewa Valley (Eau Claire, Chippewa, Dunn, Pepin counties)
- Crex Meadows Wildlife Area (ebook only)
- Douglas County
- Polk County
- Sawyer County
- Washburn County

GET CONNECTED!

Follow the author to learn about other great trails and for useful hiking tips:
- Blog: *hikeswithtykes.blogspot.com*
- Facebook: *dld.bz/fBq2C*
- Google+: *dld.bz/fBq2s*
- LinkedIn: *linkedin.com/in/robbignell*
- Pinterest: *pinterest.com/rbignell41*
- Twitter: *twitter.com/dayhikingtrails*
- Website: *dayhikingtrails.wordpress.com*

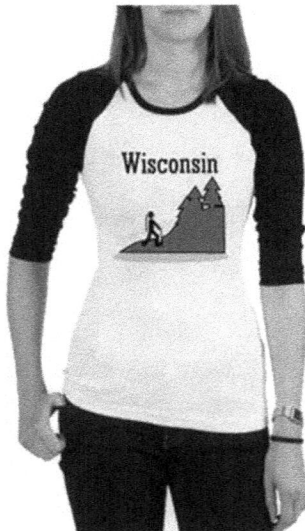

If you enjoyed this book,
please take a few moments to write a review of it at:
dld.bz/gHUzW#
Thank you!